PLATO
Statesman

CAMBRIDGE TEXTS IN THE HISTORY OF POLITICAL THOUGHT

Series editors

RAYMOND GEUSS

Lecturer in Social and Political Sciences, University of Cambridge

QUENTIN SKINNER

Professor of Political Science in the University of Cambridge

Cambridge Texts in the History of Political Thought is now firmly established as the major student textbook series in political theory. It aims to make available to students all the most important texts in the history of western political thought, from ancient Greece to the early twentieth century. All the familiar classic texts will be included, but the series does at the same time seek to enlarge the conventional canon by incorporating an extensive range of less well-known works, many of them never before available in a modern English edition. Wherever possible, texts are published in complete and unabridged form, and translations are specially commissioned for the series. Each volume contains a critical introduction together with chronologies, biographical sketches, a guide to further reading and any necessary glossaries and textual apparatus. When completed, the series will aim to offer an outline of the entire evolution of western political thought.

For a list of titles published in the series, please see end of book.

PLATO

Statesman

EDITED BY
JULIA ANNAS
University of Arizona

AND
ROBIN WATERFIELD

TRANSLATED BY
ROBIN WATERFIELD

CAMBRIDGE
UNIVERSITY PRESS

Published by the Press Syndicate of the University of Cambridge
The Pitt Building, Trumpington Street, Cambridge, CB2 1RP
40 West 20th Street, New York, NY 10011–4211, USA
10 Stamford Road, Oakleigh, Melbourne 3166, Australia

First published 1995

Printed in Great Britain at the University Press, Cambridge

A catalogue record for this book is available from the British Library

Library of Congress cataloguing in publication data

Plato.
[Statesman. English]
Statesman / Plato: edited by Julia Annas and translated by
Robin Waterfield.
p.   cm. – (Cambridge texts in the history of political thought)
Includes bibliographical references and index.
ISBN 0 521 44262 1. – ISBN 0 521 44778 X (pbk.)
1. Political science – Early works to 1800. I. Annas, Julia.
II. Waterfield, Robin, 1952–   .   III. Title.   IV. Series.
JC71.P6142   1995
321'.07 – dc20   94–18077 CIP

ISBN 0 521 44262 1 hardback
ISBN 0 521 44778 x paperback

Contents

Preface

It is perhaps appropriate for the *Statesman* to be the first of Plato's works to come out in the Cambridge Texts in the History of Political Thought; it is certainly the most neglected of Plato's political works, and the one most in need of a fresh presentation. The new translation provides a more accessible version than any hitherto available in English, and the introduction attempts to locate the dialogue in Plato's political thought, taking advantage of the enormous improvements in our understanding of this that recent discussions have produced. Few of these directly concern the *Statesman* itself, and we hope that this new translation will help to bring the work more centrally into discussions of Plato's political thought, along with the more familiar *Republic* and *Laws*.

The translation and textual notes are by Robin Waterfield, and the introduction and other notes by Julia Annas. Each of us, however, has read and commented on the other's work, and the result is the product of a harmonious collaboration that has been interesting and profitable for both of us. We hope that its fruits will introduce others to this uneven, often puzzling but seminal dialogue.

Introduction

The *Statesman* (or *Politicus*) is central to any serious concern with Plato's political thought. It clarifies and modifies Plato's earlier positions, especially in the *Republic*, and illuminates the principles of his political thinking even while these are in the process of changing.

Plato (429–347 BC) is known and discussed widely as a political thinker, but usually on the basis of his best-known work, the *Republic*, and this is in many ways a pity. The *Republic* is a work in which political theory is mixed together with ethical theory and metaphysics, and the political strand (which is not a very large one) is hard to disentangle and open to many different kinds of interpretation. Further, the political ideas, though expressed with vigour, are very sketchy, and their relation to contemporary political reality is remote. Plato's later works, *Statesman* and *Laws*, are more properly seen as works of political theory than is the *Republic*, and studying them can both help us to understand the *Republic* better, and also put it into perspective, as being only part of a long development in Plato's thinking.

In the *Statesman*, for example, Plato defends the ideal of the ruler as possessor of a particular kind of expertise, namely expertise in the 'political skill (or art)' (*politikē technē*). This idea dominates the political aspect of the *Republic*: political problems are to be solved by imposing an ideal ruler, and the only interesting question is what the nature of that rule is to be. Yet we find that, in the *Statesman*, the *Republic*'s metaphysical backing for this idea has dropped away, and that a new and far more politically relevant defence emerges. Furthermore, Plato displays a new interest in the kind of compromise that the rule of the ideal expert must make, in the real world, with laws and institutions. Likewise, while the *Statesman* does not overtly challenge the *Republic*'s view of the ideal ruler's need for both education and constraint in managing his subjects, we find that Plato has in fact considerably changed his view of the moral psychology of the citizen, and is moving towards a more egalitarian view of the relation of ruler to ruled.

Aristotle (384–322 BC), Plato's greatest pupil, responded to Plato in his own political theory as well as in other areas of philosophy. His own political views centre on the nature of political rule and what distinguishes it from other forms of authority, and it is clear from his writings that he reacts creatively to the *Statesman* both in fundamentals (for example, on the nature of political rule) and in details (for example, the framework for considering the various kinds of constitution, the 'theory of the mean'). Although Aristotle criticizes the *Republic*, in Book 2 of his *Politics*, his objections are somewhat mechanical, and it is unhelpful to compare Aristotle's work with the *Republic* rather than with the later dialogues, which Aristotle clearly found more useful as works of political thought.

However, stimulating as Plato's political ideas in the *Statesman* are, it is not surprising that the dialogue has been neglected by comparison with the *Republic* or even the *Laws*. To get to the political theory we have to go through lengthy passages which on first reading can strike us as a mixture of the boring and the weird. The *Statesman* is not only a discussion of political theory but an exercise in general philosophical method, deliberately presented as part of the same exercise as the one resulting in the theory of being and not-being in the *Sophist*. But Plato's presentation of this method has been criticized for its *longueurs*; he has abandoned the literary and attention-grabbing devices that are so plain in the *Republic*. Part of his message is now that philosophy (perhaps especially political theory) requires hard and often tedious work if we are to get it right rather than rushing (as in the *Republic*) to conclusions that may be exciting but may also be premature. Plato now stresses the need to work carefully and thoroughly through often unpromising-looking and trivial material if we are to be entitled to firm ethical conclusions. And the result has inspired far fewer readers than has the *Republic*. But, for just the same reasons, anyone who wants to get beyond the superficial grasp of Plato's political thought that comes from reading only the *Republic* should pay careful attention to the *Statesman*, as well as the *Laws*.

The dialogue is devoted to the search for a definition of the *politikos* – the possessor of *politikē technē* or the skill of ruling and organizing a political community (something for which the English 'statesman' is a pallid but unavoidable equivalent). The reason for this is something that remains constant from the earliest dialogues: to understand what we are talking about when we use a given term, rather than relying on what we pick up from other people or books and do not fully understand, we need to be able to 'give an account', to say *what it is* that we are talking about. We need to be able to do this because only if we are armed with this kind of general grasp of the field can we articulate an explanation and defence of the judgements that we make on the matter. In the early dialogues this is often given the not very happy name of a search for 'definitions'. However, what Plato is doing has little to do with definitions in our sense, and is connected rather with the demand for expert knowledge of what one is talking about.

In the *Statesman* we notice an obvious difference from the earlier kind of search, where Socrates attacks the views of others in an *ad hominem* way and generally concludes that they have learned what courage or friendship (or whatever is the object of search) is not, rather than what it is. Now the dialogue represents not the process of search but the process of exposition: the main speaker is not Socrates (who would presumably have appeared too anachronistic in this role) but an anonymous visitor from Elea, and the young interlocutor is clearly a pupil who is learning, not a partner who is contributing, negatively or positively, to the philosophical investigation. Further, we try to establish what a statesman is by narrowing down the field in a process called 'division' of wider terms. This procedure, however, is supplemented by contributions of rather different kinds: a strange myth; a discussion of the nature of illustration, and a long paradigmatic illustration of weaving; an investigation of the relationships between expertise, measurement and the trio of excess, deficiency and the 'mean'; a discussion of the different types of political constitution; and finally an account not of the statesman's nature but of one of his central political tasks, the 'weaving' of different types of people into one political fabric.

Even a casual reader is bound to be struck by the contrast between the officially organized and pedagogic nature of the discussion, and the bumpiness of the actual ride, with surprising digressions and methodological sidetracks, and a generally untidy and unfinished air to the conclusion. Scholars have divided: some think that Plato is here not in full literary control of the material, while others hold that the reader is being cued that the formally dominating structure of definition by division is not to be taken too seriously after all. Whatever the reader's conclusion about this, the *Statesman* is far less successfully unified than its official companion-piece, the *Sophist*; its different parts do in the end contribute to the understanding of a single issue, the nature of political rule, but they do so in rather diverse ways. Perhaps what we find is the result of Plato discovering that the problem of political rule is methodologically more complex and harder to expound than the nature of being and not-being.

The *Statesman* is, then, more taxing than the *Republic* to read and absorb. It is worthwhile, however, both for the light it sheds back on the *Republic* and for its interesting discussion of themes that interested Plato throughout his life.

The ruler's expertise

No reader of the *Republic* can fail to see the crucial importance of Plato's assumption there that ruling is a kind of expertise, a skill or *technē*. This is in one way merely a natural extension of the idea, prominent in the early Socratic dialogues, that virtue is a kind of expertise over one's life as a whole. In some of these dialogues (notably the *Euthydemus*, *Lovers* and *Alcibiades*) this idea is extended, without argument, to the idea that the virtuous agent will rule over others, making them, as well as himself, virtuous. However, it is the *Republic* which pushes the idea of ruling as an expertise furthest, in two ways.

One is that, although ruling is constantly compared to practical kinds of expertise like those of the doctor and navigator, Plato makes extreme demands on the theoretical competence that the rulers must have. The ruling class must spend long years doing mathematical studies, which accustom the mind to non-empirical thinking, and then study philosophy, and its supreme object, the Good, in an abstract and theoretical way. Plato never doubts that the abstract studies will improve the rulers' practical abilities, but just how this is supposed to happen is never made clear. The difficulty is made worse by the claim that people who have experienced these theoretical studies will see no value in returning to practical administration, and will have to be forced to do so.

The *Statesman*, by contrast, works out patiently and fully the differences and relationships between theoretical studies and practical applications, and corrects the picture put forward in the *Republic* on two fronts. The rulers themselves are not the ones who actually put their policies into practice; much effort is spent distinguishing their role from the instrumental roles of the different kinds of functionaries who do. The rulers' own knowledge is, by contrast, a theoretical one which guides and corrects actual practice. However, it is carefully distinguished from the type of theoretical knowledge which is *not* directive of practice – and the example given of this is mathematics; quietly, the whole basis for the Guardians' long years of abstract studies has been pulled out. We are therefore not surprised to find that the whole discussion and definition of expertise in ruling proceeds as though the central books of the *Republic* had never been written. Plato no longer thinks that political expertise requires a type of thinking which is mathematical in method and structure; as often in the later dialogues, he is rejoining common sense. He does not, however, stay there; rather, we find a quite new, and very interesting, argument to support the claims of the expert to rule, one to be discussed fully below.

The *Republic* also notoriously pushes the model of ruling as expertise in another, and more sinister direction: if ruling is really like a skill, then the people who are ruled appear to be the material for the exercise of this skill; the expert ruler would not seem to be called upon to take account of their desires and expressed preferences, since these have no standing from the viewpoint of the skill. Some of the most notorious passages in the *Republic* express exactly this view: from the point of view of rational guidance, it makes no difference if you are guided by your own reason, or by the externally imposed reason of the expert, if your own reason is not up to the task. Hence the Guardians' subjects are even called their 'slaves' (590c–d); that is, they have no autonomy over their lives where the Guardians' directives are concerned.

The *Statesman* in some passages appears to repeat and even to emphasize this aspect of the idea that ruling is an expertise (293a–b, 296b–297b): the opinions of the subjects simply do not matter, and the expert is entitled to use force to achieve his ends if necessary. The subjects may not like it, but they have no cause for rational complaint. Yet in an earlier passage (276d–e) it is explicitly made a mark of the rule of the true statesman (as opposed to the arbitrary exercise of force by a dictator) that his rule is consented to, and does not have to be imposed by constraint. The obvious internal conflict here has understandably exercised scholars. Resolution on this point is difficult, however. A relatively simple solution is to say that although the expert ruler, ruling in the interests of his subjects, would not (as opposed to the dictator who rules only for his own selfish ends) have to use constraint, this would be true only in ideal circumstances, with subjects who do not need constraint because there are no internal or external factors making it necessary. However, Plato has, since the *Republic*, developed worries about this idea too; the ideal ruler has become a problem and not just a solution to problems.

How ideal is the ideal ruler?

A large chunk of the *Statesman* is devoted to the 'myth' or story of the Age of Cronus, the traditional Golden Age when, as in the myth of Genesis, humans did not have to work or give birth and, as in other parts of the Judaeo-Christian tradition, were 'shepherded' by divine figures. Part of the point of this myth is that the expert ruler we are looking for is not the divine herdsman of the Golden Age, when the shepherd of the flock was different in kind from the flock, but rather someone whose nature is distinctively human, like the humans he rules over. In the Age of Zeus – our world – just as the world itself is now not ruled by the divine will but runs independently, by the directives of its own nature, so humans are not ruled directly by divine shepherds, but run themselves independently, by the directives of human nature, and the way they are ruled must appeal only to the human nature which is common to ruler and subjects.

This seems to be a simple and welcome point. Plato is saying that political theory should not come up with solutions which are so idealized that they have no hope of applying in the world as it is. And this is certainly what Plato's position is in the *Laws* (874e–875d) when he says that the ideal expert ruler is an unattainable ideal, since it is not in human nature to attain to expert knowledge or to remain uncorrupted by the potential for its use on other humans. When this is Plato's firm conclusion, he ceases to devote attention to the expert ruler as a solution to political problems.

But in the *Statesman* it is harder to see exactly what Plato's position is. For despite his clear application of the myth of the Golden Age, Plato continues to develop the idea that the expert ruler is the best answer to political problems, the best way to produce a state run in the interests of all. Other types of solution are, by the end of the dialogue, firmly relegated to second-best. Further, his treatment of the Golden Age myth is itself somewhat elusive. He treats the details of the traditional material in ways that are strikingly surreal, raising unavoidably the question of how seriously he is taking the idea even as a myth. And this in turn clouds the idea of just what the circumstances are which are being excluded as too ideal for relevance to actual societies.

Matters are further complicated here by the fact that the status of the myth is cloudy, too. Plato's earlier philosophical myths, in the *Phaedo*, *Gorgias* and *Republic*, are like one another in that they are recastings of traditional mythical material to serve a philosophically defensible moral and political purpose. But the *Statesman* injects a wholly new element: Plato claims that he is rationally reconstructing a story which makes sense of folk memory and folk stories. Actual Greek myths, rather than being rejected as harmful, are now regarded as fragments and shards of a larger story which is, in its outlines, true. We see here the beginnings of a much more empirical and even historical approach to political theory, one which emerges in the immense respect that Plato shows, in the *Laws*, for traditions, long-established usages and the lessons of history. But the *Statesman* myth itself wobbles between a number of genres. Which does it most resemble – the Myth of Er in the *Republic?* – the consciously fictional story of Atlantis in the *Timaeus-Critias?* – or the account of Greek prehistory in *Laws* III? The honest but uncomfortable answer is that it resembles all of them, and falls neatly into no category.

This unclarity, however, adds to the unclarity of the myth's point in the dialogue. After the *Republic*, Plato is now sure that he wants to reject over-idealized accounts of the expert ruler. But just how ideal is over-ideal? Plato has no clear answer to this difficult question, and so it is perhaps not surprising that he both clings to the thought that the truly ideal ruler would not need to use constraint, and also insists that the ideal ruler, in an unideal world, would be justified in using constraint. The source of the problems seems clearly to be that Plato is still, perhaps grimly, hanging on to the *Republic* idea that the best way to produce the best state is to install an ideal ruler, while at the same time he is developing positions that create trouble for this idea. One we have seen: political rule, to be applicable in the real world, should recognize a fundamental similarity of ruler and ruled. This is an idea which Plato takes to heart in the *Laws* and which is carried further by Aristotle. Another is increased respect for law and institutions. The *Statesman* is unstable because Plato has not yet thought through the degree of compromise that these new ideas demand.

Expertise, laws and institutions

The *Republic*, as is familiar, demands that expert rulers, the Guardians, be given a free hand and a clean slate. Although they are supposed to proceed by means of laws and regulations, this kind of regulation is regarded as obvious and trivial once the right system of education is in place, and laws do not stand in the way of the insight of the experts. The only defence of this is the lengthy description of the education itself, with its mathematical and metaphysical underpinnings.

Shorn of these, expertise needs a new defence, and in the original and interesting passage *Statesman* 292b–300e Plato provides it. What he now appeals to is the flexibility and improvisatory ability of the expert. Laws are compared to a stupid person who will not change his behaviour when new information is available because he refuses to take it in. Attaching importance to laws is like making a fetish of the rule-book in areas where rule-following is obviously self-defeating. In a sarcastic and rather funny portrayal of what we would call bureaucratic procedures Plato gives us a new argument for the importance of the expert: he achieves the goal better than the rule-follower tied up in red tape.

The weakness of the analogy is, of course, that it appeals to our responses in the case of uncontroversial skills to establish something about an expertise whose results would be highly revisionary. As in the *Republic*, Plato makes the ruler out to be a kind of doctor: you may not *like* his remedies, but you know that they are for your own good. And the problem in the analogy remains the same: it is easier for the doctor and the patient to agree on what it takes for the patient to be healthy than for the ruler and ruled to agree on what measures the ruled should be subjected to.

But two rather interesting things happen at this point. One is that *this* argument for expertise quite patently falls far short of justifying constraint. The more we appeal to the intuitive idea that we would rather see the doctor than just renew his prescription, the less intuitive seems the idea that the doctor is therefore entitled to *force* his new prescription on us. This is another idea that Plato comes to accept later. In the *Laws* (720a–e, 857c–e) the analogy of the doctor appears yet again, and this time the point about constraint is explicitly recognized. It is only doctors to slaves who can impose their remedies; a free person is entitled to demand that the doctor explain the need for the remedy and persuade the patient to submit to it. In the *Laws* Plato has taken the point that citizens are not relevantly like slaves to their rulers, however expert; and expertise, however superior to the rule-book, is no longer taken to justify constraint.

The other point is that the *Statesman* argument for the superiority of expertise to law brings with it its own correction; the rule-book is not as good as the doctor's own personal judgement, but it is a lot better than nothing, or guesswork, or, worst of all, obedience to a charlatan. Laws are a second-best to the ideal expert; but if you lose interest in the ideal expert as a solution, laws do not look as irrelevant as the *Republic* made them out to be. The less interesting the prospect of an ideal ruler, the more pressing it becomes to turn one's attention to averting anarchy and tyranny; and in the section on the different types of constitutions we find Plato turning to a more realistic and common-sense appraisal of the actually available political options in the Greece of his time.

Four points stand out from Plato's discussion of the different types of constitutional arrangement. The first is that the definitions are realistic; they converge with common sense and ordinary political discourse. In this they contrast strongly with the discussion of different types of state in Books 8 and 9 of the *Republic*, where the account of the different states is strongly driven by the analogy of soul and state, and often bears no obvious relation to contemporary reality. The most striking example of this is that of democracy, where in the *Republic* Plato is pushed by the analogy of soul and state to say very peculiar things. Given his account of the soul, the 'democratic' personality has to be a person in whom desires are dominant; and desires are directed solely at their own satisfaction, with no regard for the overall good of the whole person. The 'democratic' personality has no way of ranking his desires; hence he pursues serious and trivial concerns with equal commitment. Correspondingly, the 'democratic' state has to be one in which every member counts for as much as every other, and no 'élitist' differentiations are allowed. Plato follows this idea through in extreme ways – women are equal to men, pupils to teachers, etc. – which bear no relation to any democratic state he can have known about, certainly not Athens (562d–563d). In the *Statesman*, by contrast, Plato, unencumbered by the soul-state analogy, classifies states in a sensible and common-sense way: are the rulers one, few or many? The rule of the many, in all its forms, is democracy. All the *Republic*'s unreal problems drop away at a stroke, and Plato looks more dispassionately at the advantages and disadvantages of democracy in the real world. Not for nothing was Aristotle deeply influenced by this passage.

Secondly, Plato is freed by this newly sensible approach to give a newly sensible evaluation of democracy. Instead of berating it for occupying a low rank in his own system, he actually looks at the way it functions. The main feature he picks out is that, as a system of government, it is weak, because it parcels out authority more widely than others do. This, of course, renders it open to the accusations of comic bureaucracy that Plato is ready to make. But there is another side to this. A system that makes it difficult for the virtuous to take control and impose their expertise is also a system that makes it difficult for the vicious and selfish to take control and impose their own views and interests. Plato, for the first time, realizes that the feature of democracy that makes it most resistant to the rule of 'true kings' in ideal circumstances is actually an advantage in the real world, since it also makes it most resistant to dictatorship, and in the real world there are more potential dictators than potential true kings.

Plato can never bring himself to be really enthusiastic about democracy, not even in the *Laws*, where his ideal state takes over huge amounts of Athenian democratic institutions. But in the *Statesman* we see him for the first time realizing the advantages of democracy from the viewpoint of a realistic assessment of how political institutions actually function.

Thirdly, it must be admitted that Plato's interest in actually functioning political factors is somewhat uneven. In the passage at 291e we find him cross-dividing the three forms of rule (one/few/many) by three criteria, namely whether the form of rule receives consent or not, whether it is by the rich or poor and whether laws are respected or not. However, in the later passage which refers back to this (302b–303b) only the third of these criteria is mentioned. Plato, on the verge of asking a number of significant questions, is sidetracked by concern with expert knowledge and its relation to law, and loses interest. We find Aristotle, in passages of the *Politics* (1279a22–1280a6, 1289a26–b26, especially 1289b5–6, which seems to be a reference to the *Statesman* passage) taking up and consciously improving on Plato's analysis here.

Finally, Plato's main interest in this passage is the one which emerges at the end, namely the importance of laws and institutions. In an imperfect world (and few have thought the actual world more imperfect than Plato) it is better to stick rigidly to one's laws than to allow tinkering. In the *Republic* (425c–427a) this kind of tinkering was ridiculed because it falls so far short of the comprehensive rational ideal. In the *Statesman* the reason is more down-to-earth: the tinkering is likely to be in partisan and selfish interests, whereas established laws are more likely to express collective wisdom. Plato is on the way to the almost Burkean reverence for tradition and established custom that we find in the *Laws*. He has come to see law, however rigid, as expressive of what a community has agreed on, and, just as such, having some status as against the desires of particular people to alter it.

It is remarkable that a community's consensus should, just as such, have any rationally defensible status for Plato, especially when we consider the uncompromising stance in many of the early dialogues against the force of majority opinion. And once again we find a point which is accepted in the *Laws*, but which has a murkier status in the *Statesman*. For here it is not just any old consensus which has authority, but shared *true* opinion, and it is the expert ruler, not just tradition, which is charged with bringing this about. This takes us on to the issue of the *Statesman*'s view of the ordinary citizens and their attitudes.

The moral psychology of the citizen

Very little is said in the *Statesman* about the state which the ideal ruler will rule, or its citizens. However, the passage at the end about weaving the fabric of the state, though technically it is not part of the dialogue's official task of defining the statesman, is another original and seminal passage in Plato's political thought.

It seems to be assumed that the citizens subject to the ideal ruler will be subjected, as are the citizens in the *Republic*, to an overall system of education and training. (The theme of force and constraint, emphasized earlier, drops out in this passage, where the stress is all put on the effects of education.) But the extreme differences of nature between types of citizen, on which Plato lays such enormous stress in the *Republic*, are no longer apparent. Plato still thinks that the rational ability needed to produce a ruler is not one that could be widespread among people, but, in keeping with his earlier recognition of the essential similarity of ruler and ruled, he has dropped the hierarchical class-system that is such a feature of the *Republic*. Two noteworthy results of this are likely to strike the reader.

Firstly, all the citizens must, as far as possible, be unified by the 'divine bond' of true belief held securely about basic matters of right and wrong (309c). It is of course not new for Plato to hold that most people can have merely true belief whereas only the expert ruler has knowledge, but the emphasis has shifted somewhat. No longer a second-rate means for making sure that most people do what the Guardians deem best for them, the beliefs of the citizens are, when they converge on the truth, something divine. And it matters that the citizens hold these beliefs *securely*; Plato is softening his earlier line that stability is a mark of knowledge, while beliefs are unstable. The status of true belief has shifted upwards; we are on our way to the even more revisionary position of the *Laws*, where Plato holds that we use our minds, the spark of divinity in us, in conforming ourselves to the laws, which are the product of human reasoning working in the past. In the *Statesman* he is not yet prepared to assign such an approved status to tradition.

The other surprise for the reader in these final pages is an explicit defence of the view that the virtues, in an agent, do not naturally tend towards unification, so that intervention is needed to ensure that the citizens all have the virtues in a unified form. Plato is not actually denying that the virtues, in their completed form, imply one another. But he is claiming that people naturally come in two types, each of which tends to go to undesirable extremes, and that this must be checked by the opposite character type to produce the desirable, virtuous result, which will not tend to extremes. The checking is done partly by insisting on intermarriage and partly by education.

There is much that is understated or not worked out in the passage, notably the connection of the courageous and moderate types with quickness and quietness. But it is clear enough that Plato is moving towards some version of the theory of the 'mean', raised already in the earlier passage 283c-285c, and worked out in more careful detail later by Aristotle. Roughly, the natural material for virtue in people has a tendency to develop in one of two opposed, but equally undesirable ways, and it takes rational intervention, in the form of education, to produce true virtue, which is a 'mean' between the undesirable extremes.

In Plato these ideas remain sketchy. But it is significant that he is now prepared to recognize deep differences of character among ordinary people. And the differences that interest him sound a new note, one that will again find larger development in the *Laws*. Plato, aware of a long and depressing history of Greek states waging aggressive wars against other Greek states, is intensely concerned that citizens of his ideal state be able to defend themselves – and that means, he recognizes, being soldiers as excellent as any fourth-century mercenaries: they must be thoroughly trained in courage, endurance and the soldierly excellences. On the other hand, he regards it as disastrous for a state to foster only aggressive and militaristic virtues in its citizens. The many bitter criticisms of Sparta in the *Laws*, echoed by Aristotle, show that he was aware of the dangers in creating a soldierly society. In the *Republic* he tries to meet this problem by ensuring that the psychology of the Guardians will be both courageous and restrained. In the *Laws*, faced by the problem in the case of all the citizens, he tries hard to have it both ways, to create a society of trained warriors who are unmilitaristic, whose main citizenly virtue is the traditionally feminine one of *sōphrosunē*, sobriety and self-control. The *Statesman* does no more than start this idea going, and it notably fails to meet any of the associated problems, such as the role of women.

The self-imposed framework of the *Statesman* does not permit these issues to be developed. However, it did not prevent Plato earlier turning aside to myths, weaving and other matters; so the truncated nature of the discussion cannot be explained by the form of the dialogue alone. Perhaps – this is no more than a suggestion – Plato felt that he would not be in a position to develop these ideas until he had given a satisfactory account of the nature of political rule in its new context, without a supporting metaphysical background. And, as we have seen, his attempt to do that turns out to lead him into new and fruitful thoughts – thoughts, however, which cast more and more doubt on the viability of the *Statesman*'s central retention of the importance of political expertise.

The *Statesman* is in some ways a record of complication and even confusion. But not only does it help us to see how we get from the *Republic* to the *Laws*, it is a record of the entanglements that only a very great and original thinker, defending and qualifying his boldest work at the same time, could get into.

The dialogue form

All Plato's works are in the form of dialogues in which he is not a speaker. One obvious reason for this way of writing (as startling to Plato's contemporaries as to us as a way of writing philosophy) is to detach Plato, the writer, from the arguments presented, and, in particular, from the conclusions reached. Plato never presents his own position; he just shows us people arguing. The arguments, the discovery of their premises and the evaluation of them and of their conclusions, are for us to develop. (And this is what generations of Plato scholars have always done.)

The matter is complicated, of course, by the fact that in the Socratic and middle-period dialogues the main speaker is Socrates, who is clearly presented as an exemplary philosophical figure, in contrast to the stupid, mediocre or malign people who argue with him. However, even Socrates usually argues *ad hominem* in the early dialogues; he argues against the positions of others, never directly to support claims of his own. And the character Socrates argues for such a variety of positions in different dialogues, and in such different ways, that the relation of the Platonic Socrates to Plato remains deeply disputed.

The later dialogues in a way simplify matters; for Socrates, though often present in the company which gathers at the start of a dialogue, retires as the main interlocutor in favour of the nameless visitor from Elea, or Timaeus or Critias. In the *Laws* he is not even present. But it would, I think, be a mistake to think that whereas the earlier Socrates is opaque, these figures are nothing but mouthpieces for Plato's own views. Even when there is no interesting characterization, Plato uses these figures always to distance himself formally from the argument. The argument is, by means of these figures, presented to the reader, as in the earlier dialogues. Readers, however, almost inevitably feel that in these later dialogues the distancing has somewhat lessened, especially in view of the overt pedagogical form of a dialogue like the *Statesman*. The dialogue form seems less appropriate, not only because these dialogues are less entertaining but because Plato's need to distance himself from the main line of argument and its conclusions has also shrunk. We get the point that the argument is presented to us as an argument for us to engage with, and not just as Plato's view; but this point is easily taken, and we can be left somewhat wearied by the continuation of the convention of conversation.

However, there is a further point: the convenience of the dialogue form, given the numerous occasions when the thread of discussion is interrupted or obscured by material that one would not hitherto have taken to be relevant – a myth or a definition of weaving. The dialogue form retains the convenience of pragmatic flexibility: a prose treatise on the subject of the *Statesman* could not have displayed so handily its many shifts of concern and insertion of different kinds of material. Retaining the distancing effect of the dialogue form enables Plato to develop the dialogue as he wants, rather than settling for a genre like the prose treatise which brings its own rules and expectations with it. To the end, Plato values technical means which both give him maximum control over the way he writes, and leave the reader a task of working things out. It is still true in the *Statesman* that this task is not limited to filling in the blanks in a pre-set pattern, but takes up the demand to continue the argument, following it where it leads.

Translator's note

In preparing this translation, the Oxford Classical Text (E.A. Duke, W.F. Hicken, W.S.M. Nicoll, D.B. Duke and J.C.G. Strachan, eds., *Platonis Opera*, vol. I, Oxford University Press, 1994) has been followed, except in the few places indicated in the notes. We are extremely grateful to David Robinson for letting us see a copy of the text of *Statesman* in advance of publication.

The canonical essay on Plato's style of writing in his later dialogues remains the General Introduction by Lewis Campbell to his 1867 edition of *Sophist* and *Statesman* combined (see the bibliography on pp. xxviii–xxix). Here I need only point out to the reader that the Greek of *Statesman* is occasionally difficult and dense, and that it rarely rises to the conversational fluency and brilliance of Plato's early and middle-period dialogues. At the same time, he sometimes experiments – for no very good reason that I can see – with artificial alliteration, word order and rhythm. It is in the nature of translating from one language to another that these rhetorical devices are likely to be lost: they certainly have been in the following translation. Otherwise, my intention has been to keep as close to the Greek as a reasonable degree of fluency allows, without losing the occasionally dry and laborious tone of the original. Apart from this tone, however, there is little in the way the dialogue has been written to deter a potential reader, and (as always in Plato) enough thought-provoking material to make a reading worthwhile. If this translation revitalizes the dialogue for new generations of readers, it will have done its job.

Chronology of principal events

469	Socrates born
429	Plato born
399	Socrates executed
384	Aristotle born
380–370s	At some point, Plato begins to hold formal instruction in the Academy gymnasium; this develops into the Academy as a philosophical school, about whose institutional structure we know almost nothing.
367	Aristotle joins the Academy
347	Plato dies

Other events in Plato's life mentioned in the ancient biographies are of doubtful chronology, and often doubtful historicity.

The chronology of Plato's dialogues is very uncertain, but on stylistic and other grounds there is general agreement that the *Statesman* belongs with the latest group of dialogues, written at a time when Plato was teaching in the Academy.

Bibliography

Other relevant Platonic dialogues are *Crito* (translated by G. Grube in *Plato, Five Dialogues*, Hackett, 1981), *Republic* (translated by R. Waterfield, Oxford University Press, 1993) and *Laws* (translated by T. Saunders, Harmondsworth, 1975).

Ackrill, J.L., 'In Defence of Platonic Division', in *Ryle*, ed. O.P. Wood and G. Pitcher (London, Macmillan, 1970), 373–92

Blundell, S., *The Origins of Civilization in Greek and Roman Thought* (Beckenham, Croom Helm, 1986)

Bobonich, C., 'The Virtues of Ordinary People in Plato's *Politicus*', forthcoming in Rowe (ed.)

Campbell, L., *The Sophistes and Politicus of Plato* (Oxford, Clarendon Press, 1867)

Diès, A., *Platon, Le Politique* (Paris, Les Belles Lettres, 1935)

Gill, C., 'Plato and Politics: The *Critias* and the *Politicus*', *Phronesis* 24 (1979), 148–67

Guthrie, W.K.C., *A History of Greek Philosophy V: The Later Plato and the Academy* (Cambridge, Cambridge University Press, 1978), ch. II (4)

Klosko, G., *The Development of Plato's Political Theory* (New York and London, Methuen, 1986), ch. XI

Mohr, R., *The Platonic Cosmology* (Leiden, Brill, 1985)

Owen, G.E.L., 'Plato on the Undepictable', *Exegesis and Argument: Studies presented to Gregory Vlastos* (Assen, Van Gorcum, 1973), 349–61

Rowe, C. (ed.), *Reading the Statesman: The Proceedings of the Third International Symposium Platonicum* (Academia Verlag, forthcoming)

Saunders, T., 'Plato's Later Political Thought', in R. Kraut (ed.), *The Cambridge Companion to Plato* (Cambridge, 1992), 464–92.

Skemp, J.B., *Plato, The Statesman* (London, Routledge and Kegan Paul, 1952)
revised by Martin Ostwald, *Plato's Statesman* (Indianapolis/Cambridge, Mass., Hackett, 1992)

Taylor, A.E., *Plato: The Sophist and the Statesman* (London, Nelson and Sons Ltd., 1961)

Tomasi, J., 'Plato's *Statesman* Story: The Birth of Fiction Reconceived', *Philosophy and Literature* 14 (1990), 348–58

Biographical note

SOCRATES of Athens, 469–399. Philosopher who wrote nothing, and devoted his life to philosophical discussion; executed on a religious charge. He inspired Plato, Xenophon, Aeschines, Antisthenes and others to make him the protagonist in philosophical dialogues. He appears in all of Plato's dialogues except the *Laws*, but in the later dialogues retires as the main interlocutor.

YOUNG SOCRATES of Athens. Member of the Academy.

THEODORUS of Cyrene, born 460. Pupil of Protagoras; well-known mathematician. Young Socrates and Theaetetus are presented as his pupils in the *Theaetetus*.

THEAETETUS of Athens, 414–369. Mathematician and philosopher, pupil of Theodorus and member of the Academy. He takes no part in the dialogue of the *Statesman*, but is presumably present as a silent listener, having played the role of answerer to the Visitor from Elea (the role taken here by Young Socrates) in the companion dialogue *Sophist*.

VISITOR FROM ELEA. Generally regarded as an invention of Plato's. Elea was the home-town of the philosophers Parmenides and Zeno; this is more relevant to the theme of the companion dialogue *Sophist* than it is to the theme of the *Statesman*.

Statesman

SOCRATES: I'm really very grateful to you, Theodorus, for intro- 257a
ducing me to Theaetetus. And thanks for the introduction to our
visitor as well.[1]

THEODORUS: You'll probably be three times as grateful, though,
Socrates, when they've completed their portraits of the statesman
and the philosopher as well.

SOCRATES: All right – *if* this is what you want us to report as
the view of our foremost arithmetician and geometer, Theodorus.

THEODORUS: What, Socrates? b

SOCRATES: That he counted each of the men as equivalent, when
their relative values progress by leaps that are too great for you
mathematicians with your ratios.

THEODORUS: That's a good point, Socrates. I call on Ammon,
the god of my race,[2] to witness that I admit it. You're quite right

---

[1] The characters are Socrates, Theodorus of Cyrene (a well-known mathematician),
an unnamed visitor from Elea, and Young Socrates, a member of Plato's Academy.
The opening conversation links the dialogue to (i) the *Theaetetus*, where Socrates
meets the young Theaetetus and Young Socrates, pupils of Theodorus, and has a
long discussion with Theaetetus about knowledge, (ii) the *Sophist*, where Theodorus
introduces to Socrates the visitor from Elea, who in dialogue with Theaetetus
presents a solution to the Eleatic (deriving from Parmenides of Elea) problem of
being and not-being. In the *Statesman* Socrates again meets Theodorus and the
Eleatic visitor, who this time takes Young Socrates as his partner. The formal
framework linking the three dialogues is very artificial, since the *Theaetetus* is
methodologically very different from the other two. This opening passage indicates
that Plato intended to write a fourth dialogue, in which the Eleatic visitor would
give a definition of the philosopher, to follow those of the sophist and statesman.
No such dialogue has come down, and it seems that Plato abandoned the project
(as he abandoned the project of following the *Timaeus* with two other dialogues).

[2] Theodorus, from the Greek city of Cyrene in North Africa, is identifying the local
god Ammon with the Greek god Zeus.

to tell me off for my mathematical mistake.³ Thanks for the reminder. I'll get my own back on you another time, but for now I'd like to ask our visitor to continue his kindness and next to pick either the statesman or the philosopher, whichever he likes, and
c give us an account of him.

VISITOR: Yes, I'd better, Theodorus. I mean, once we've undertaken a project, we oughtn't to give up until we've reached the end. But what should I do about Theaetetus here?

THEODORUS: What do you mean?

VISITOR: Shall we give him a break and instead get Socrates here to join us in our exertions? What do you suggest?

THEODORUS: Yes, I agree with you: get Socrates involved instead. When you're young, as these two are, all you need is a break and then you can easily cope with all kinds of hard work.

d SOCRATES: And that's not all. There's a sense in which they both might be said to be related to me. At any rate, you all say that one of them looks like me;⁴ and the other is my namesake –
258a our names bring us into some kind of relationship. Now, relatives like us should always be happy to use conversation to get to know one another. The discussion I myself had with Theaetetus yesterday brought us together, and I've also listened to him answering you just now. On the other hand, I haven't seen Socrates in either role. I ought to see what he's made of as well, though, so I think you should put your questions to him now, and I can do so later.

³ Socrates has pedantically taken up Theodorus' casual assertion that he will be 'three times as grateful' for the definitions of sophist, statesman and philosopher as he would be for only one of them. He criticizes this for the assumption that all three are equal in value, whereas the value of the philosopher is so much greater than that of the statesman (and that of the statesman than the sophist) that they cannot be put into a mathematical ratio at all. Why is Socrates, of all people, criticizing a leading mathematician? Perhaps the point is that a philosopher, even if not a mathematician, is competent to criticize the assumptions that a mathematician makes.

The object of the current investigation is the 'statesman', *politikos*, the person taken to have knowledge of and competence in political matters (literally, the affairs of the city-state or *polis*). It is assumed, and never discussed, that the possessor of such knowledge will be a ruler, i.e. someone whose knowledge is expressed in organizing the political life of others. We can see from the *Republic* that for Plato the nature of ideal political rule is the central issue in political theory, and the *Statesman*'s starting-point makes best sense as directed to an audience already familiar with the *Republic*.
⁴ Theaetetus; cf. *Theaetetus* 143e.

2

VISITOR: All right. So, Socrates, do you hear what Socrates is suggesting?
YOUNG SOCRATES: Yes.
VISITOR: And do you agree with him?
YOUNG SOCRATES: Yes, I do.
VISITOR: It doesn't look as though *you*'re going to put any b obstacles in our way, and it would presumably be even less appropriate for *me* to. Anyway, I think we ought to investigate the statesman next, now that we've finished with the sophist. Tell me: do you think we should or should not count him as another one of those people who are in possession of a branch of knowledge?[5]
YOUNG SOCRATES: I think we should.
VISITOR: So we'd better make distinctions between the various branches of knowledge, as we did before when we were looking into the sophist.
YOUNG SOCRATES: I imagine so.
VISITOR: But I don't think it'll take the same division as before, Socrates.[6]
YOUNG SOCRATES: No?
VISITOR: No, it'll take a different one.   c
YOUNG VISITOR: I suppose so.
VISITOR: Where will we find the path that leads to the statesman, then? I mean, that's what we have to do. We have to track statesmanship down, differentiate it from all other branches of knowledge by assigning it to a single identificatory category, and count all the rest as belonging to some other single category. Then we can get our minds to think of all branches of knowledge as falling into two categories.[7]

---

[5] Note the unargued assumption, right at the start, that the statesman or *politikos* is the possessor of knowledge. *Epistē. .ē*, the Greek word for knowledge, has a plural which is difficult to render in English; we are forced to use 'branches of knowledge' and the like. Plato assumes that we can use *epistēmē* interchangeably with *technē*, skill or expertise; he refers to the opening of the *Sophist*, which divides *technai*.

[6] *Sophist* 219a ff. begins by dividing kinds of expertise into acquisitive and productive (later a third, separative, is added).

[7] It is assumed without discussion that the right way to characterize the statesman and to say what he is, is to employ a method of 'cuts' or 'division', in which, starting from more general characterizations, one homes in on (metaphors from hunting and tracking down are frequent here) the desired notion by cutting off irrelevant parts of the concept at hand. At *Phaedrus* 265c–266b Socrates says that one must first 'collect' widely scattered notions that belong under a single wider

YOUNG SOCRATES: I'm already pretty sure that I'm not up to the task. You'll have to do it.

d VISITOR: Yes, but as things become clear to us, Socrates, you must join in as well.

YOUNG SOCRATES: That's fair.

VISITOR: All right, then. Would you say that mathematics and similar disciplines have nothing to do with action? That *all* they provide us with is knowledge?

YOUNG SOCRATES: Yes.

VISITOR: Whereas the kind of knowledge which is involved in building and manual work in general is more or less essentially e involved with action and assists these disciplines in their realization of physical entities which formerly did not exist.

YOUNG SOCRATES: Of course.

VISITOR: So this gives you a criterion for differentiating between branches of knowledge in general. You can distinguish knowledge which is practical from knowledge which is purely theoretical.

YOUNG SOCRATES: All right. I agree to your distinction of these two categories within the single field of knowledge.

term, and only then 'divide' to reach a satisfactory characterization, in a way that is like dividing a carcass into its natural joints instead of merely hacking bits off. In the *Sophist* and *Statesman*, however, we start by dividing; presumably 'collecting' is the preliminary work which is not relevant to displaying the finished product. Division results in establishing a single 'class' or 'category' of what is sought; the words here translate *eidos* and *idea*, often translated 'form'; and the process of division clearly takes on, in a more low-key way, many of the issues earlier discussed in more metaphysically loaded contexts. The present search for forms or categories continues to assume that there are objective natural forms or kinds, which we discover and whose existence does not depend on our conventions; and that we discover these through the philosophical use of reasoning. In this respect there is a continuity between the *Statesman* and the Socratic 'dialogues of definition'. Aristotle regards the process of 'division' into two parts at each stage as a crude kind of definition by genus and differentia, and criticizes a version of it in chapters 2 and 3 of the first book of *The Parts of Animals*. Plato's own practice is loose and variable; in the *Sophist*, for example, several definitions by division of the sophist are produced. In the *Statesman*, although the attempt to produce a definition by division of the statesman formally provides the framework of the dialogue, many other different kinds of contribution to our understanding are made which have nothing to do with division. 'Division' in Plato's later dialogues functions rather like 'analysis' in some modern discussions: it can suggest more precision than is actually employed, but it clearly refers to a characteristic mode of doing philosophical discussion.

VISITOR: Now, do you think the statesman, the king, the slave-master, and the estate-manager too all belong to a single category, or do you think there are as many areas of expertise here as there are names?[8] Perhaps it would be better if you were to consider the matter from the following point of view.

YOUNG SOCRATES: What?

VISITOR: Imagine a person who, despite holding no official position, is qualified to act as an adviser to one of the state physicians. Wouldn't we have to use the same professional title in referring to him as we would when referring to the person whose adviser he is? 259a

YOUNG SOCRATES: Yes.

VISITOR: What about a person who, again despite holding no official position himself, is qualified to advise the king of some country or other? Won't we say that he has the knowledge which, by all rights, the king himself ought to have?

YOUNG SOCRATES: Yes.

VISITOR: Now, the knowledge a true king has is kingship. b

YOUNG SOCRATES: Yes.

VISITOR: And whether a person with this knowledge is in fact a ruler or an ordinary citizen, it will be perfectly correct – as long as we're thinking about just his expertise, anyway – to say that he has what it takes to be a king.

YOUNG SOCRATES: Yes, that would be fair.

---

[8] Here is an initial emphatic commitment on Plato's part to the idea that the areas named are merely different areas of application of what is itself one single expertise. Aristotle's denial of this forms a fundamental point of disagreement in political theory; he denies exactly this assertion at *Politics* 1252a7–23, clearly with the present passage in mind. For Aristotle there is a basic difference between exercise of authority over inferiors, and political rule, which is distinguished by being exercised over those who are 'equal and similar' to oneself; hence it is appropriate in a political community to 'rule and be ruled' in turns. Here Plato rejects such a difference in kind (though he regards ruler and ruled as far less different than they are in the *Republic*). Note also that here Plato introduces an equivalence between the statesman and the king. (This also happens abruptly at *Euthydemus* 291b.) In view of the normal Greek association of kingship with foreign and arbitrary rule ('the king' normally meaning the king of Persia) this is an indication that familiarity with the *Republic* is presupposed, 'king' standing in for ideal rulers like the Guardians. (Plato connects the two uses shortly.)

VISITOR: If we put statesmanship and kingship and their respective practitioners into the same category, then, we do so on the grounds that they're all the same, don't we?

YOUNG SOCRATES: Obviously.

VISITOR: And there's no difference between an estate-manager and a slave-master.

YOUNG SOCRATES: No, of course not.

VISITOR: Well, as far as their government is concerned, is there any difference between a large estate with its pretensions and a small state with its pomp?

YOUNG SOCRATES: None at all.

c VISITOR: So the answer to our present question is obvious: all these cases involve a single branch of knowledge, which could be called 'kingship' or 'statesmanship' or 'estate-management'. We won't mind in the slightest which of these titles is used.

YOUNG SOCRATES: Of course not.

VISITOR: Another obvious point is that what any king can contribute towards the maintenance of his authority manually and by physical means in general is very little compared to what he can do with intelligence and strength of mind.

YOUNG SOCRATES: Yes, that's clear.

VISITOR: So shall we say that a king's affinities lie more with
d theoretical knowledge than with the kind which is manual and basically practical?

YOUNG SOCRATES: I'm sure we should.

VISITOR: What if we go on to make distinctions within theoretical knowledge? Would that be the next thing for us to do?

YOUNG SOCRATES: Yes.

VISITOR: Now, if you look carefully, you might be able to spot a natural joint within theoretical knowledge.[9]

YOUNG SOCRATES: Where?

e VISITOR: I'll tell you. You know the branch of knowledge we call arithmetic.

YOUNG SOCRATES: Yes.

VISITOR: It's undoubtedly a branch of theoretical knowledge, surely.

---

[9] The image is of dividing up a carcass into joints; cf. *Phaedrus* 265e. The visitor returns to the question of natural divisions at 262c ff.

YOUNG SOCRATES: It certainly is.

VISITOR: Now, when an arithmetician notices a difference between certain quantities, we expect him to evaluate the difference, but we don't expect his function to go beyond that, do we?

YOUNG SOCRATES: Of course not.

VISITOR: And then there's the master builder. No master builder is an actual workman; he's an overseer of workmen.

YOUNG SOCRATES: Yes.

VISITOR: What he provides is not manual labour, but knowledge.

YOUNG SOCRATES: Exactly.

VISITOR: It would be right, then, to say that he possesses theoreti- 260a
cal knowledge.

YOUNG SOCRATES: Yes.

VISITOR: But in his case, I think, it would be inappropriate for him just to evaluate, and then stop and leave it at that, as our arithmetician did. He has to tell each of the workmen what to do and see that they carry out his instructions.

YOUNG SOCRATES: That's right.

VISITOR: So although it and all similar branches of knowledge are theoretical, and although all the disciplines which depend on arithmetic are as well, nevertheless there's a difference between these two categories in the sense that one evaluates and the other b
issues instructions. Yes?

YOUNG SOCRATES: I think so.

VISITOR: So suppose we break theoretical knowledge as a whole down into two parts, and call them 'instructional' and 'evaluative'. Would that be a reasonable distinction to make?

YOUNG SOCRATES: I'm sure it would.

VISITOR: Well, it's always nice for partners to agree.

YOUNG SOCRATES: Of course.

VISITOR: And as long as we're partners in our current venture, we won't bother with others' opinions.

YOUNG SOCRATES: Why should we?

VISITOR: Now then, in which of these two areas of expertise c
should we locate kingship? Is a king a spectator of some kind, in which case we should place him in the evaluative category? Or would it be better for us to count him as knowing how to issue instructions, since he does after all exercise authority?

7

YOUNG SOCRATES: It would definitely be better for us to do that.[10]

VISITOR: We'd better take a look next at expertise in issuing instructions, then, and find a way to break it down. I think I can see how. I think we can distinguish between kings and heralds in

d exactly the same way as we do between retailers and producer-sellers, who sell their own produce.

YOUNG SOCRATES: What do you mean?

VISITOR: What retailers do is take over other people's produce and re-sell it, when it's already been sold once.

YOUNG SOCRATES: Yes.

VISITOR: And what heralds do as well is take over other people's ideas, which they've received in the form of instructions, and deliver exactly the instructions they were given all over again to a different set of people.

YOUNG SOCRATES: You're quite right.

VISITOR: Well, should we bracket what kings do with what a

e large number of other people do – translators, bosuns, diviners and heralds, for instance? After all, they all issue instructions. Or shall we follow the analogy we came up with a moment ago and make up an equivalent name, since there isn't really an accepted name, in fact, for people who issue their own instructions?[11] Then we can divide the group in question along these lines, and put kings into a 'producer-instructional' class. As for all the rest, we can ignore them and leave it to someone else to find a different name for them, because the purpose of our enquiry is to track

261a down the ruler and we aren't interested in any non-rulers.

YOUNG SOCRATES: I agree.

---

[10] Note that arithmetic is put into the evaluative, purely theoretical part of theoretical knowledge, separately from kingship, which is theoretical knowledge that has implications for practice. This is one striking sign that Plato has abandoned the *Republic*'s assumption that years of training in abstract mathematics is needed for the ruler's expertise. Plato returns to the relationship of directive theoretical knowledge to practice at the end of the dialogue (303e–305e).

[11] Here Plato makes a virtue of indifference to actual usage; even though we are working through low-key examples, we are not concerned to map common sense, but to produce a rationally defensible account of what we are seeking. At 261e he makes the point that philosophers should not quibble over words (cf. *Republic* 454a, *Theaetetus* 177d-e, *Sophist* 218c).

VISITOR: Now that we've adequately separated these two groups, by distinguishing between what comes from others and what originates with oneself, the next task is to subdivide the producer-instructional class, isn't it? I mean, we have to see if it contains a crack that we can open up.

YOUNG SOCRATES: Yes.

VISITOR: And I think it does, but you should join me in opening it up.

YOUNG SOCRATES: Where?

VISITOR: Won't we find that the reason that any ruler – any conceivable kind of ruler – issues instructions is to produce results? b

YOUNG SOCRATES: Definitely.

VISITOR: Now, it's hardly difficult to divide things in general into two distinct classes.

YOUNG SOCRATES: How?

VISITOR: Some things are inanimate, and some are alive.

YOUNG SOCRATES: True.

VISITOR: Well, this distinction will help us in our attempts to divide the instructional aspect of theoretical knowledge.

YOUNG SOCRATES: How?

VISITOR: We can assign to one part the work of producing results in the inanimate sphere, and to the other part the work of producing results in the sphere of living creatures. That will immediately give c us an exhaustive division of the class as a whole.

YOUNG SOCRATES: It certainly will.

VISITOR: Now, one of these parts needn't concern us, but we should take the other and treat it as a whole to be divided into two.

YOUNG SOCRATES: Which of the two parts do you think we should take?

VISITOR: The one which issues instructions in the sphere of living creatures, of course. I mean, a king can hardly be said to exercise his authority over inanimate objects, as a master builder does. No, he has a higher role: he works with living creatures and functions d exclusively in that domain.

YOUNG SOCRATES: You're right.

VISITOR: Now, there are two aspects to producing results and looking after things in the sphere of living creatures. You find people either taking care of single creatures, or being responsible for them collectively in herds.[12]

YOUNG SOCRATES: Right.

VISITOR: But we're surely not going to find statesmen maintaining individual creatures, as drovers or grooms do; stock-farmers of horses and cattle are a closer analogy.

YOUNG SOCRATES: I'm sure you're right, now that I hear it said.

e VISITOR: So what shall we call the collective maintenance of a number of living creatures at once? Shall we call it 'herd-maintenance' or 'collective maintenance'?

YOUNG SOCRATES: Whichever of these names crops up as we talk.

VISITOR: Well said, Socrates. If you can retain this relaxed attitude towards terminology, your stock of wisdom will increase as you get older. For the time being, however, let's do as you suggest. But can you find a way to show that herd-maintenance is divisible? That would enable us to concentrate our search on half the ground

262a in future, instead of trying, as we are now, to locate our quarry in an area which is double the size it might be.

YOUNG SOCRATES: I'll do my best. I think there's a difference between the maintenance of human beings and the maintenance of beasts.[13]

VISITOR: That was a very decisive and courageous effort at division. But we mustn't let this happen to us again, if we can help it.

YOUNG SOCRATES: We mustn't let what happen again?

VISITOR: We must beware of singling out just one small part and contrasting it with a number of large parts, and of doing so without

b any reference to classes. Any part we distinguish must also constitute a class. If one's quarry can legitimately be distinguished from

---

[12] The characterization of political communities as 'herds' may bring to mind some of the more alarming talk of herds and breeding in the *Republic*. (Even apart from this, it is a demeaning characterization; members of religious congregations have sometimes resisted the authoritarian implications of the idea that they form a 'flock'.) Here, however, it is just an implication of the idea that the ruler is a kind of herdsman or shepherd; as this idea is modified so is the idea that citizens are a kind of herd.

[13] The idea that humans are not merely a flock is not rejected, but the visitor refuses to take this as an obvious step. It has to emerge from further definition and the interpretation of the myth; otherwise we could not be sure that we had found a real form, rather than the result of an artificial distinction.

everything else at a single stroke, that's wonderful – that's what you were trying to do a moment ago. You saw that the discussion was heading in the direction of human beings, you thought you had the division within your grasp, and so you rushed the discussion. But delicate work is tricky, my friend. It's safer to proceed by making an incision down the middle: you're more likely to meet with true categories that way – and the importance of that for analysis cannot be overestimated.   c

YOUNG SOCRATES: I don't quite see what you mean.

VISITOR: I like you, Socrates, so I'll try to explain. A thorough explanation is out of the question at the moment, but I'd better try to clarify things by taking the matter a little further forward.

YOUNG SOCRATES: Well, perhaps you could explain what mistake I was making when I was trying to categorize things just now.

VISITOR: All right, here's an analogy. Suppose one wanted to divide the human race into two parts. What most Greeks do is d
make the division by separating Greeks from all the rest: they use the single term 'barbarian' for all the other categories of people, despite the fact that there are countless races who never communicate and are incompatible with one another, and then expect there to be a single category too, just because they've used a single term.[14] Or here's another example, of someone thinking he's dividing quantity into two classes. Suppose he takes the number 10,000 on its own and treats it as a distinct class of quantity, and then e
makes up a single name for all the rest of the numbers; the use of the name might make him regard that category too as a single class, different from his first one. A better division, of course – one which forms a true division into two distinct classes – would be to divide quantity into odd and even, or to divide the human race into male and female.[15] But Lydians or Phrygians or any other

[14] 'Barbarian' literally means someone whose language one does not understand. The visitor's point is that this does not pick out a *unified* class; various peoples are not brought into a single natural grouping by the fact that they are not comprehensible to Greeks, and an important sign of this is that some of them are not comprehensible to one another. Here it is particularly clear that a category or form requires there to be an objective natural kind with its own principle of unity, not an artificial construction.

[15] The second example also produces two parts neither of which has a naturally unifying principle; note that Plato holds that gender division, unlike linguistic divisions (and presumably the ethnic divisions underlying these) does give naturally unifying principles.

group should only be separated and contrasted with everyone else when it's impossible to find that either of the two parts one has 263a isolated is a class, rather than just a part.

YOUNG SOCRATES: You're quite right, but the crucial question is how one can become familiar enough with 'class' and 'part' not to confuse them but to see that they are different.[16]

VISITOR: That's a very good question indeed, Socrates, but a complex one to answer. We've already strayed quite a long way from the matter at hand, and here you are encouraging us to stray even further! I think we should probably return to the interrupted b discussion for now; if there's time later we'll follow the tracks of the problem you've raised. However, it's essential for you not to fall into the trap of thinking that my account constitutes a clear exposition of the issue.

YOUNG SOCRATES: What account?

VISITOR: When I said that classes and parts are different.

YOUNG SOCRATES: What of it?

VISITOR: Any class is bound also to be a part of whatever it's being said to be a class of, but a part is not similarly bound to be a class. That's what I was getting at, Socrates, so please don't ever think I meant that things could be the other way round.

YOUNG SOCRATES: All right.

c VISITOR: Now, here's the next question for you to answer.

YOUNG SOCRATES: What?

VISITOR: What was the point which initiated our digression and brought us here? I seem to remember that it was when you were asked how to divide herd-maintenance and you answered very decisively that there are two categories of creatures, one consisting of human beings and the other a unit consisting of all other beasts.

YOUNG SOCRATES: That's right.

VISITOR: And it was clear to me at the time that you were isolating a part, and then thinking that all the creatures you were left with formed a single class simply because there was available d to you a single name, 'beasts', which you could apply to them all.

YOUNG SOCRATES: Yes, that's right too.

---

[16] Both Young Socrates and the visitor focus on the easy issue, whether class and part are distinct; nothing is said as to how the enquirer can ascertain whether she has found a class or a mere part, doubtless because Plato thinks that there is no general answer to this. In each case there is no substitute for rational investigation.

VISITOR: Despite your courage, however, my friend, you should consider the following possibility. Imagine another species which is endowed with intelligence, as cranes are supposed to be (or you can imagine some other species, if you prefer), and imagine them undertaking the same task of distributing names as you; they might exaggerate the importance of their own species by making cranes into a single class to contrast with all other species, and they might lump together all other creatures, including humans – and what else would they call them but 'beasts'? So let's try to avoid that e kind of mistake.[17]

YOUNG SOCRATES: How?

VISITOR: It's less likely to happen if we don't take the class of creatures as a whole and try to divide it.

YOUNG SOCRATES: No, I suppose we shouldn't.

VISITOR: No, because that's how the mistake occurred earlier.

YOUNG SOCRATES: Go on.

VISITOR: We found that within theoretical knowledge there was a part of it which issues instructions and is concerned with the maintenance of creatures, and specifically with the maintenance of gregarious animals, didn't we?

YOUNG SOCRATES: Yes.

VISITOR: Well, even then we already had available to us the 264a division of the category which consists of all creatures into tame and wild. Creatures capable of being domesticated have long been called tame, while those which aren't are called wild.[18]

YOUNG SOCRATES: That's a good point.

VISITOR: Now, the domain of the branch of knowledge we're trying to track down is and always has been tame creatures – not forgetting that we expect to find that it's concerned with gregarious animals.

YOUNG SOCRATES: Yes.

VISITOR: So we don't need to take the complete range of creatures into consideration when we make our division, but we also shouldn't rush at it and try to reach statesmanship in a hurry. That's already b made us experience what the proverb says happens.

YOUNG SOCRATES: What's that?

---

[17] The example of the cranes (jokingly brought in as intelligent birds) adds a new point: an artificial grouping, answering to no division in nature, may be merely the result of the projection of an attitude on the part of the divider. The application to the Greek use of 'barbarian' is obvious.

[18] Reading ἔχοντα with MSS. BT.

VISITOR: Our haste has made us achieve less speed in making our divisions.

YOUNG SOCRATES: It's a good thing it has.

VISITOR: You might be right. Anyway, let's try to divide collective maintenance all over again. It's possible that by the end of the argument you'll have a clearer view of what you're after. Here's a question for you.

YOUNG SOCRATES: What?

VISITOR: Well, I'm sure you've never actually been there yourself,
c but there's something I wonder whether you might have heard about from others – that there are tame fish in the Nile, and that the Persian king also has some in ponds. It's just possible that you've seen some in people's fountains.

YOUNG SOCRATES: I've certainly seen them here, and I've often heard about the ones abroad as well.

VISITOR: And even if you've never actually been around the plains of Thessaly, you must have heard reliable reports of how people keep geese and cranes there.

YOUNG SOCRATES: Of course.

d VISITOR: The reason I'm asking you all these questions is that there are two kinds of creatures which are kept in herds: some live in water and some on dry land.

YOUNG SOCRATES: True.

VISITOR: Do you also agree that this gives us an appropriate method for dividing this branch of knowledge, collective mainten-ance? We can allocate these two kinds of creatures to the two segments of collective maintenance, and then call one segment 'water-based maintenance' and the other 'land-based maintenance'.

YOUNG SOCRATES: Yes, that seems fine to me.

VISITOR: And we don't need to ask which of these two areas of
e expertise kingship falls under, because it's absolutely obvious.

YOUNG SOCRATES: Of course it is.

VISITOR: Now, anyone could divide the land-based division of herd-maintenance.

YOUNG SOCRATES: How?

VISITOR: By distinguishing between creatures with wings and those with feet.

YOUNG SOCRATES: You're quite right.

VISITOR: And the search for statesmanship should obviously

concentrate on the domain of creatures with feet, shouldn't it?[19] Don't you think that anyone with even the tiniest amount of intelligence would think that?

YOUNG SOCRATES: Yes.

VISITOR: So we'd better find a way to treat the art of herding creatures with feet like an even number and halve it.

YOUNG SOCRATES: Obviously.

VISITOR: Now, there seem to be two roads stretching ahead of us here, either of which will take us to the subsection which is the goal of our discussion. One path, which is a short cut, involves separating a small segment from a large one; the other conforms more closely to the principle we enunciated earlier, of cutting as close as possible to the middle, but would take longer. We can proceed down whichever of these two paths we want.   265a

YOUNG SOCRATES: Can't we take them both?

VISITOR: Are you suggesting that we take them both at once, Socrates? That would be a remarkable feat! But obviously we could take them in turns.

YOUNG SOCRATES: I vote for taking them in turns, then.   b

VISITOR: That won't be difficult, because there isn't a great deal left to do. It would have been a hard instruction to comply with if we were at the start of our journey or were halfway through it. In fact, though, since this is what you want to do, I suggest we take the longer route first,[20] because the journey will be easier while we're still relatively fresh. Tell me what you think of my divisions.

YOUNG SOCRATES: I will when I hear what you have to say.

VISITOR: There's a natural dichotomy within all gregarious, tame creatures with feet.

YOUNG SOCRATES: What?

VISITOR: Some have horns and some lack horns.

YOUNG SOCRATES: I should say so.   c

VISITOR: Now, when you divide expertise at herding creatures with feet and assign the appropriate content to each division, you'd better use an expression, because any single terms you could come up with would be too unwieldy.

YOUNG SOCRATES: What kind of expression?

---

[19] Reading <δῆλον> ὡς περ<ί> (Waterfield).
[20] There is no reason not to read προτέραν with all the older MSS.

VISITOR: You could say, for instance, 'In dividing the branch of knowledge which is the herding of creatures with feet, we have allocated one part to gregarious creatures with horns and the other to those without horns.'

d YOUNG SOCRATES: The way you've put it is perfectly clear, so let's allow this expression of yours to stand.

VISITOR: And it's also obvious that a king herds creatures which have been cropped – which lack horns, I mean.

YOUNG SOCRATES: Of course it is.

VISITOR: Let's try to break down this hornless herd, then, and assign to the king what we find to be his.

YOUNG SOCRATES: Yes.

VISITOR: Shall we divide it according to whether the creatures' hoofs are split or, in technical terminology, uncloven? Or shall we divide it according to whether they interbreed or breed only with their own kind? Do you understand what I'm getting at here?

YOUNG SOCRATES: What?

e VISITOR: That horses and asses can bear each other's offspring . . .

YOUNG SOCRATES: Yes.

VISITOR: While no other tame, gregarious, hornless creatures can interbreed.

YOUNG SOCRATES: Of course they can't.

VISITOR: Well then, do you think a statesman is responsible for managing creatures which interbreed or creatures which breed only with their own kind?

YOUNG SOCRATES: Obviously creatures which cannot interbreed.

VISITOR: So, to continue with the method we've been employing, I suppose we'd better divide this category in two.

YOUNG SOCRATES: Yes.

266a VISITOR: But by now we've chopped up almost the full range of tame, gregarious creatures; only two species remain, since dogs don't really deserve to count as gregarious animals.

YOUNG SOCRATES: No, they don't. But what criterion shall we use to distinguish the remaining two?

VISITOR: A criterion which one might expect you and Theaetetus to use, since you're interested in geometry.

YOUNG SOCRATES: What is it?

VISITOR: The diagonal, and then the diagonal of the diagonal!

YOUNG SOCRATES: What do you mean?

VISITOR: Consider our nature as human beings. How are we b equipped for walking? Isn't it just like the diagonal which can be raised up to two feet?

YOUNG SOCRATES: Yes, exactly!

VISITOR: And then consider the nature of the other species. It is the diagonal of our human diagonal, since it can be raised up to twice two feet!

YOUNG SOCRATES: Of course! And yes, I have a pretty good idea what you're getting at.

VISITOR: And that's not all, Socrates. Can you see that, as a result of all our dividing, something else has happened which might make c people laugh and so go down well with them?

YOUNG SOCRATES: What's that?

VISITOR: The human race has been paired and kept pace with the most noble and easy-going of creatures.

YOUNG SOCRATES: Yes, I can see that. What a strange thing to happen!

VISITOR: Well, isn't it fair for the slowest creatures to be the *pig*gest failures at running?[21]

YOUNG SOCRATES: Yes, all right!

VISITOR: And here's an even more amusing consequence. Do you realise that, in running along with his herd, the king has also kept up with people who have trained hard for the easy life? d

YOUNG SOCRATES: You're quite right.

VISITOR: You see, Socrates, this is a particularly clear case of something that came up before, in the *Sophist*.

YOUNG SOCRATES: What?

VISITOR: That the relative prestige or humbleness of something is entirely irrelevant to the kind of logical enquiry we're engaged in. This kind of enquiry doesn't sneer at trivial things and prefer important things; for its purposes, it is concerned only with the truth at every stage.

---

[21] A far-fetched joke, not worth the carriage. There is also a pun on *pous*, 'foot', which is used both as a mathematical measure and as a part of the body. The pig is potentially four-footed as humans are potentially two-footed. (See J.B. Skemp, *Plato, The Statesman* and *Plato's Statesman* for the mathematical details.) The only point here is to provide material for the following remark: we should not be put off by low-key examples, for trivial content may be very important for ascertaining the method that will lead to important conclusions. (The *Sophist* reference is 227b-c. Cf. the earlier *Gorgias* 491a.)

YOUNG SOCRATES: I suppose so.

VISITOR: Now, shall I next take the shorter route we came across
e before to the definition of the king, to save you having to ask me
about it?

YOUNG SOCRATES: Yes, please.

VISITOR: I think what we should have done then is break creatures
with feet down immediately into a two-footed category and a four-
footed category. We'd have seen that human beings are paired only
with winged creatures, and we would then have divided gregarious
two-footed creatures into a feathered category and a featherless category. This would have made the art of herding human beings clearly
visible, and we could then have taken the statesman-king and insti-
tuted him as the charioteer, so to speak, of this art. We could have
handed over the reins of the state to him, seeing that this branch of
knowledge is rightfully his.

267a YOUNG SOCRATES: Thank you for your account. It settles what
we might call your debt to me, and by adding an account of this
alternative route, you've also paid the interest in full.

VISITOR: Now then, shall we go back over the argument from start
to finish and trace the thread of what is entitled to be called statesmanship?

YOUNG SOCRATES: Yes.

VISITOR: Well, we started by taking theoretical knowledge and
distinguishing an instructional part of it, and we then drew on an
analogy to make up the term 'producer-instructional' for a further
b subdivision. Next, within this 'producer-instructional' branch we
isolated the not unimportant art of maintaining creatures. We found
that a category of creature-maintenance was herd-maintenance, and
that a category of herd-maintenance in its turn was the herding
of creatures with feet. Within the herding of creatures with feet,
the crucial segment we distinguished was the art of maintaining
those which lack horns. And if you want to encapsulate in a single
term the relevant subdivision of this art of maintaining creatures
which lack horns, you have to combine at least three components
and call it the branch of knowledge which is concerned with 'the
herding of species which cannot interbreed'. As for subdividing
c this class, since the art of herding human beings is the only
section left which deals with two-footed gregarious creatures, then

it is exactly what we were after – the art we've been calling both kingship and statesmanship.[22]

YOUNG SOCRATES: That's a perfect summary.

VISITOR: Is what we've done really what you've just said it is, Socrates?

YOUNG SOCRATES: What?

VISITOR: I'm not sure we *have* given a perfectly adequate account of the matter under consideration. I'm wondering whether the main deficiency in our enquiry might not be precisely that although some kind of definition has been given, the picture is *not* perfectly complete. d

YOUNG SOCRATES: What do you mean?

VISITOR: For both our sakes, I'll try to clarify my thoughts.

YOUNG SOCRATES: Yes, please.

VISITOR: Well, didn't we find a short while ago that there are a number of arts which count as herding, one of which is statesmanship, which is responsible for managing one particular kind of herd?

YOUNG SOCRATES: Yes.

VISITOR: And the branch of knowledge which our argument defined as statesmanship was the collective maintenance of human beings, as opposed to the maintenance of horses or any other animals.

YOUNG SOCRATES: Yes.

VISITOR: Well, I think we should note a respect in which kings e differ from other herders.

YOUNG SOCRATES: What?

VISITOR: Do any of the others have rivals who, despite going under different professional titles, maintain that they are qualified to look after the same herd as well?

YOUNG SOCRATES: What do you mean?

VISITOR: Think of any merchant, farmer or miller, for instance; think of trainers and doctors as well. I'm sure you're aware that they would all take issue with our people-herding statesmen, and would come up with all kinds of arguments to insist that responsibility for 268a

---

[22] The definition so far appears not only ludicrous in itself but of dubious relevance to political theory. It acquired a certain fame in antiquity as an object of ridicule, though usually in extremely inaccurate versions, defining humans as two-footed, etc. animals receptive of political expertise rather than focusing on political expertise itself. (Cf. Sextus Empiricus, *Outlines of Pyrrhonism* II 28, *Adversus Mathematicos* VII 281–2; cf. the pseudo-Platonic *Definitions* 415a.)

maintaining human beings is *their* concern, and that they aren't limited to just the common run of people, but are actually responsible for the rulers as well.

YOUNG SOCRATES: And they'd be right, wouldn't they?

VISITOR: Perhaps. We'd have to think about that, but what we already know is that this kind of dispute never arises in the case of cattle-herders. A cattle-farmer maintains his herd by himself, doctors them by himself, acts as a kind of go-between in their love-affairs by himself, and when they're in labour, with offspring to be brought into
b the world, he and he alone supplies expertise in midwifery. And that's not all: these animals do have a limited capacity for taking their ease and responding to music, and there's no one better than he at calming them down and charming them into docility. No one else can supply his herd with music as well as he can, whether he plays instruments or sings with no accompaniment. And the same goes for all other animal-herders, doesn't it?

YOUNG SOCRATES: You're quite right.

VISITOR: I don't see, then, how we can consider our definition of
c a king accurate and incorrigible. We've made him our expert in herding and maintaining the human herd, when there are countless others disputing his claim and all we've done is concentrate on him rather than them.

YOUNG SOCRATES: No, it can't be correct.

VISITOR: We were right to be worried a short while ago, then. We suspected that, although we'd certainly described a king in outline, we wouldn't have a portrait of the statesman that was complete in all its details until we'd stripped away the surrounding horde, with their rival claims to maintain the same herd, and made him stand out on his own, separate from his rivals and untainted by their qualities.
d YOUNG SOCRATES: You're quite right.

VISITOR: Then that's what we'd better do, Socrates, if we want to avoid an account which would in the final analysis be flawed.

YOUNG SOCRATES: We certainly ought to avoid that.[23]

VISITOR: We'd better go back to the beginning, then. And this time we ought to find a different starting-point and adopt a different approach.

---

[23] The fault in the definition is not that it does not accurately pick out the statesman, but that it does so in a way that cannot yet be adequately defended against

YOUNG SOCRATES: What?

VISITOR: We should make room for a bit of light relief, as it were, and help ourselves to a lengthy fragment of a major myth, before returning for the rest of the discussion to the previous method of separating one part from another and gaining the summit we're after e that way. Do you think that's a good idea?

YOUNG SOCRATES: Yes.

VISITOR: So pay very careful attention to the myth, then, as if you were a child listening to a story. In any case, you haven't left child-hood far behind yet.

YOUNG SOCRATES: Please go on.

VISITOR: Among the ancient tales which have often been repeated and will continue to be told in the future as well, the particular event I'm thinking of is the miracle which occurred at the time of Atreus' and Thyestes' famous quarrel. I'm sure you're familiar with the story and remember what's supposed to have happened.

YOUNG SOCRATES: Presumably you mean the portent of the golden lamb.

VISITOR: No, I mean the change that took place in the rising and 269a setting of the sun and the other heavenly bodies. It's said that in those days they used to set where they rise nowadays, and rise on the opposite side of the earth, and that God changed things over to their present configuration then, as an act of testimony for Atreus.[24]

YOUNG SOCRATES: Yes, that's part of the story too.

VISITOR: There are also a lot of stories about Cronus' rule and kingdom.

---

objections. Hence the broadening of scope with the myth, which in fact leads to a major change in the definition.

[24] A golden lamb growing in the herd of Atreus gave him the right to be king; his jealous brother Thyestes seduced Atreus' wife and thus gained possession of the lamb, but to support Atreus' claim Zeus caused the heavenly bodies to change their courses. The visitor appeals to this and to other current mythical material to support his claim that folk-memory and myth preserve fragments of a true account of the history of the cosmos. This marks a striking change in Plato's attitude to Greek myth, previously dismissed as largely misguided and harmful. The long narrative, mythical in form, that follows rationalizes elements in Greek myth, but is also clearly Plato's invention, not all of it regarded with equal seriousness. It seems to be a piece of Platonic irony, for example, that the functioning of our world, which we find natural, is from the cosmic point of view a case of something running backwards. For the use of traditional materials about the origins of humankind, see Blundell (1986). For details of the cosmological elements, see Skemp (1952) and Mohr (1985). For suggestions about the myth's genre and comparison to the Atlantis story in *Timaeus-Critias* see Tomasi (1990).

b YOUNG SOCRATES: 'A lot' is an understatement.

VISITOR: And it's also said that in the old days people used to be born from the earth, rather than from other human beings.

YOUNG SOCRATES: Yes, that's another of the things we're told used to happen in ancient times.

VISITOR: Well, all these things are a result of the same incident. In fact, they're the least remarkable of all the countless consequences of this incident, but because it all happened such a long time ago, the other events have either been forgotten, or have been split up, with their various parts now forming separate stories. None of the stories tells of the incident which caused all these events, however,

c but I'd better do so, because it will help us in our attempt to understand kingship.

YOUNG SOCRATES: That's a very good idea. Do please tell us the story, and don't leave anything out.

VISITOR: All right. Periodically, this universe of ours is under the guidance of God himself; at these times he helps it on its circling way, but there are also times – when it has spun around for the appropriate amount of time – when he releases it. It then revolves back again in the opposite direction under its own impulse, since it

d is a living creature and has been granted intelligence by its original constructor. There's a particular reason why this ability to retrace its path is bound to be an inherent part of its make-up.

YOUNG SOCRATES: And what is this reason?

VISITOR: Only the most divine entities have the property of remaining for ever in an unchanging, self-identical state, and any material thing is not of this order. However, although the creator of what we call heaven or the cosmos granted it a great many enviable qualities, it is at least partially material, and therefore it

e is impossible for it to be completely free from change. Nevertheless, in so far as it is within its power to do so, it keeps to the same place and restricts the change it undergoes to a single, stable form of motion. So the reason it has the ability to revolve in the opposite direction is that this reversal is the smallest possible alteration of its former motion. There is nothing which is always the source of its own motion, except perhaps the initiator of all motion, and it would be blasphemous to suggest that *this* moves at different times in opposite directions. All this rules out three notions: first, that the cosmos is always the source of its own motion; second, that it is always God who is turning the cosmos as a whole, in both of its conflicting directions; third, that its movements are due to a 270a pair of gods with conflicting purposes.[25] Then the only position we're left with is the one we've just formulated: that the universe is sometimes helped on its way by a divine cause external to itself (and during this period its maker renews its life and replenishes its store of immortality), while at other times it is released and moves under its own impulse. And it is let go at precisely the right moment to enable it to retrace its path for hundreds of thousands of cycles, thanks to its enormous mass, its perfect balance, and the tiny 'foot' it uses for travelling.[26]

YOUNG SOCRATES: Your whole account sounds very plausible b to me.

VISITOR: I wonder if it provides a basis for understanding, after some thought, the incident which, I suggested, caused all those remarkable things to happen. I'll tell you exactly what the incident in question was.

YOUNG SOCRATES: What?

VISITOR: Consider the fact that the universe sometimes revolves in the direction it is currently taking, but sometimes goes in the opposite direction.

YOUNG SOCRATES: What of it?

VISITOR: A number of reversals take place in the heavens, but it's impossible to think that any of them involve the kind of extensive c and wholesale change that this one does.

YOUNG SOCRATES: That seems likely.

VISITOR: So we're also bound to think that this is the time when we inhabitants of the universe experience the most extreme changes.

YOUNG SOCRATES: That seems likely too.

VISITOR: But it goes without saying that it's hard for living creatures to endure a large number of extensive and various changes when they happen all at once.

YOUNG SOCRATES: Of course.

VISITOR: So this is bound to be a time when creatures in general suffer widespread destruction, and when the human race in particu-

---

[25] This is dubiously consistent with *Laws* 896c, which seems to assert a cosmic dualism of a good and an evil cosmic soul.

[26] Talk of the world's 'foot' or pivot is somewhat peculiar. Presumably it is a way of saying that very little friction is generated.

d lar is all but wiped out. A lot of remarkable and extraordinary things happen to the survivors, but one, which is a consequence of the unwinding of the universe that occurs when the reversal of its present direction occurs, is particularly important.

YOUNG SOCRATES: What is it?

VISITOR: At first, every living creature stayed just as old as it was and every mortal thing stopped getting older in appearance; then they all went into reverse and started growing younger, as it

e were, and softer! Old people's white hair darkened; bearded men's cheeks became smooth and regained the lost bloom of youth; as the days and nights passed, young people's bodies became smoother and smaller and they reverted to a state which was no different, mentally as well as physically, from infancy; then their bodies, which were by now fading fast, just completely disappeared. And the corpses of people who met with violent deaths during this period went through exactly the same changes in a short space of time, so that within a few days their bodies had deteriorated and

271a vanished.

YOUNG SOCRATES: But how were creatures born in those days? How did parents produce offspring?

VISITOR: Quite simply, Socrates, they didn't: there was no such thing at that time as parental procreation. It was the earth-born race, whose existence once upon a time we hear of in our stories, which was born: that was the time when they began to rise up again out of the earth. Our earliest ancestors, who were the immediate

b neighbours in time of the end of that former cycle, though they were born at the beginning of the present cycle, left records of the existence of the earth-born race. They passed these stories on to us – stories which are nowadays commonly disbelieved, although they don't deserve to be. You have to look at the matter from a particular point of view and then you can understand it, I think. I mean, it's in keeping with the idea of old people turning into children that people would reform in the earth where they were lying after their death and would come back to life from there, in conformity with the reversal undergone by all natural cycles. Any people who were not gathered up by God for some other destiny,

c therefore, necessarily formed an earth-born race in this way. That is why they're called 'earth-born', and that's the origin of the legend.

YOUNG SOCRATES: Yes, this is perfectly consistent with the earlier parts of your account. But you also mentioned life under Cronus' regime.[27] Did this happen when the heavenly bodies had reversed the direction they took before, or the direction they take now? I mean, it goes without saying that a change in the motion of the sun and the heavenly bodies takes place during both reversals.

VISITOR: You've followed the discussion well. As for your question, there isn't the slightest trace in the current cycle of things d just happening without people having to put in any effort; this is another feature of the former cycle. You see, in the first place, God oversaw and was responsible for the actual rotation as a whole in those days, and the same thing happened domain by domain as well,[28] with the parts of the cosmos being exhaustively divided between various tutelary gods. To take living creatures in particular, a different divine spirit was assigned to every species and every flock, to act as its herdsman, so to speak. Each spirit had sole responsibility for supplying all the needs of the creatures in his charge. As a result, there was no such thing as creatures preying e on one another or savagery in general, and fights and disputes were completely unknown. Thousands of examples could be given of other consequences of this arrangement, but here are the reasons for the stories about people living an effortless life. God himself was directly responsible for managing the human herd, just as nowadays humans herd inferior species because they are closer to godhood. With God as their herdsman, there was no organized society, no marriage and no children (because everyone just came 272a back to life out of the earth, with no memory of their past lives). But even if these kinds of things played no part in their lives, trees and other plants produced huge crops and grew in abundance, without needing to be farmed: the soil yielded them of its own accord. People spent most of their time roaming around in the open air without clothes or bedding, since the climate was temperate and caused them no distress, and the earth produced more than enough grass for them to lie on in comfort. That's what I have to b

---

[27] The Age of Cronus, father of Zeus who overthrew him, is the traditional location of the Golden Age. As in the traditional accounts, Plato makes this an era without need for work, and without sexual relations and reproduction, though his way of doing this is not very serious.

[28] Reading ἄλλως δὲ κατὰ τόπους . . . πάντῃ (Waterfield).

tell you, Socrates, about life under Cronus: our present life, which is supposed to be under Zeus, you know about at first hand. But are you able, or are you inclined, to decide which of the two ways of life makes people happier?

YOUNG SOCRATES: No, I couldn't.

VISITOR: Shall I find a criterion for assessing them?

YOUNG SOCRATES: Yes, please.

VISITOR: As well as having so much spare time, Cronus' wards had the ability to communicate with animals as well as human beings; so the crucial issue is whether they used all these advantages c of theirs for philosophical purposes. If they entered into discussions with animals as well as one another, and if, whenever they found that a given species had a particular talent, they tried to learn in what unique way it could add to their understanding, then it's an easy decision: they were infinitely happier than people nowadays. If, on the other hand, they stuffed themselves with food and drink and had the kinds of conversations with one another and with the animal species that we hear about these days in our stories, then d again, from my point of view, it's easy to decide about their relative happiness.[29] Still, let's drop this topic for the time being, until we come across someone who can give us reliable information about which of the two attitudes people in those days held about knowledge and which of the two purposes they made conversation serve. We'd better turn to the reason for bringing up this myth of ours, so that we can make progress and complete the next phase of our account.

Eventually, this whole set-up had lasted as long as it was meant to and there had to be a change; the whole earth-born race had e been used up, since every soul had fulfilled its quota of incarnations and had fallen to earth as seed as often as had been ordained for it. Then the helmsman of the universe released the tiller, so to speak, and withdrew to his vantage-point, and both fate and its innate longing made the universe start to move backwards. As soon as all the gods who had deputized for the supreme spirit in the

---

[29] Here Plato's didactic and moralizing side comes through: the traditional pictures of the Golden Age must be quite mistaken if they represent people as happy in a totally unintellectual state.

various domains of his kingdom realized what was happening, they
too stopped supervising their sections of the cosmos. 273a

The universe had been impelled in a direction which opposed
the one it had come from and was tending towards, so it recoiled
and crashed against itself. This caused a series of immense shocks
to pass through it, and these shocks annihilated, yet again, all kinds
of living creatures. Subsequently, once enough time had passed,
the chaos and disturbance ended, the shocks died down and the
universe was at peace. Normality and order were restored to its
path. It had power and responsibility for itself and all its parts,
and did its best to remember the injunctions it had been given by b
its father-maker. At first, it carried out his commands quite exactly,
but later – due to the fact that at least some of its components
were material – some precision was lost, because before attaining
its current ordered form as the cosmos, materiality (which is a
primordial and inherent aspect of the universe) was steeped in a
great deal of disorder. The point is that all the good there is in
the universe stems from the constructor of the universe, whereas
cruelty and injustice – in so far as they are features of the universe – c
stem from the disorderly condition it used to be in; the universe
would not include these qualities, nor would it breed them in its
creature, had it never been in that condition. While the universe
was under the helmsman's influence, then, it used to engender
little bad and plenty of good in the creatures it maintained within
its boundaries. But then the helmsman departs. In the period
immediately following this release, the universe continues to keep
everything going excellently, but as time goes by it forgets his
injunctions more and more. Then that primeval disharmony gains
the upper hand and, towards the end of this period, the universe
runs riot and implants a blend of little good and plenty of the d
opposite, until it comes close to destroying itself and everything in it.

When God, who organized the universe, sees the dreadful state
it has got itself in by this stage, he is concerned. He doesn't want
to see it swept away and wrecked by the storms of chaos, to
founder in the infinite sea of dissimilarity. And that is why he e
resumes his place at the helm and puts it on a new tack, away
from the corruption and decomposition it had been steering for
under its own impulse in the preceding cycle; that is why he

organizes it again, corrects it and makes it immortal and ageless once more.

There is nothing more to be said on this, but if we take up the previous part of the tale, that will help us in our attempt to understand kingship. You see, once the universe had been set on the path towards the way things are today, the process of ageing again came to a standstill and produced another series of extraordinary phenomena – the opposite phenomena from those which had happened before. Creatures which were so small that they were just about to vanish began to grow; bodies which had just been born from the ground with grey hair died and returned to the earth. What was happening to the universe was being repeated and
274a reproduced in the changes everything was undergoing, and in particular the process of pregnancy, birth and child-rearing conformed of necessity to the general pattern. The point is that creatures could no longer develop inside the earth as a result of various elements coming together and combining, so it was ordained that all the constituent parts of the universe should do their best to propagate and give birth and maintain their offspring by themselves, because this conformed to and was part of the same tendency which ordained that the universe as a whole should be responsible for its own course.

b   We have now reached the point we were aiming at all along in this tale. It would be a long, complicated matter to explain how and why all the other animals changed, but it won't take long to describe what happened to human beings, and that will be more relevant to our purposes. Now, we had previously been maintained by a spirit, whose flock we were, but then this spirit's supervision was removed. At the same time, most animals became wild, because they were innately fierce, and started to prey on the weak – and
c now defenceless – human race. In these early days, human beings had not yet developed their tools and skills; they had been used to being maintained without having to do anything themselves, but now they were deprived of that; they didn't yet know how to provide for themselves, since no need had ever forced them to learn in the past. As a result of all this, they were in a very bad way indeed. That is why the gods gave us the gifts we hear about in the ancient tales, along with the necessary education and training – fire from Prometheus, the crafts from Hephaestus and the

goddess who shares his skill,[30] seeds and plants from others. This ᵈ
is the origin of everything which contributes towards the totality
of human life, following the event I recounted a moment ago when
we were deprived of divine supervision and had to start fending for
ourselves and being responsible for ourselves, just as the universe as
a whole did. In conformity and in keeping with the rhythms of the
universe, we swing for all time this way and that in our lives and
in the means of our birth. Anyway, I think we should end the ᵉ
myth there and start to put it to work. It will help us see how far off
the mark we were in our earlier description of the statesman-king.

YOUNG SOCRATES: Where did we go wrong? How far off the
mark do you think we were?

VISITOR: From one point of view, we didn't fall far short of our
target, but from another point of view we were way off and it was
a far more substantial error than I thought it was.

YOUNG SOCRATES: What do you mean?

VISITOR: Well, we were asked to define the statesman-king from
the current cycle, from the way things are today, but in our reply
we spoke of the shepherd of the human flock; but he belongs to 275a
the opposite cycle, and is divine rather than human, so from this
point of view we were way off the mark. Then there's also the
fact that we described him as ruling over a state as a whole, but
failed to explain *how* he rules; from this point of view, what we
said may have been incomplete and unclear, but it was at least
true, so this mistake is less serious than the other.

YOUNG SOCRATES: Right.

VISITOR: So what we have to do, I suppose, is define how a
statesman rules over a state, and then we can reasonably expect
to have a complete description of him.

YOUNG SOCRATES: Yes, that's a good idea.

VISITOR: But that's why we introduced the myth as well. It wasn't ᵇ
supposed just to show that everyone disputes our current quarry's
claim to herd-maintenance; we also wanted to get a clearer view
of whoever actually is the one and only person who (on our model
of shepherds and cowherds) should properly take responsibility for
maintaining the human herd and therefore should be regarded as
deserving the name of statesman.

[30] Athena.

YOUNG SOCRATES: Right.

VISITOR: But a mere king, I think, is too slight to fit into our
c outline of the divine herdsman, Socrates. It wouldn't be particularly
easy to distinguish one of today's statesmen here on earth from
their subjects, in terms of their natures, and they had more or less
the same education and upbringing.

YOUNG SOCRATES: Yes, that's undeniable.

VISITOR: Still, it shouldn't make the slightest bit of difference to
the amount of effort we devote to tracking him down whether he's
divine or human.[31]

YOUNG SOCRATES: Of course it shouldn't.

VISITOR: So let's resume our investigation. Here's a fresh starting-
point. We took the branch of knowledge which deals with creatures
in a 'producer-instructional' way and which is responsible for managing them collectively rather than individually, and we called it
d (without further ado at the time) 'herd-maintenance'. I'm sure you
remember, don't you?

YOUNG SOCRATES: Yes.

VISITOR: That was pretty much where we went wrong, because
the statesman simply wasn't there for us to trap or label. We were
so busy with names that we didn't notice him making his escape.

YOUNG SOCRATES: What do you mean?

VISITOR: It's only *other* herders who are concerned with maintaining their herds. The statesman isn't, so we should have found
a label which applies equally to all herders, and used that rather
e than subsuming him under herd-maintenance.

YOUNG SOCRATES: Yes, you're right, if there actually is such a
label.

VISITOR: But surely we could have said that they all equally *tend*
to creatures, even without having distinguished whether they do so
by maintaining them or by doing anything else, couldn't we? At
the point in the argument when it was clear that we had to find
a term which encompassed the statesman as well as all the rest of
them, we could have used 'herd-management' or 'herd-tendance'
or even something like 'herd-responsibility' as the generic label.
Any of these would have done.

---

[31] But the application of the myth makes an important difference: the ruler we are
looking for is not different in kind from his or her subjects either in nature or
in upbringing. We are not to look for an unrealistically ideal ruler.

YOUNG SOCRATES: You're right. And then what would the next 276a division have been?

VISITOR: We'd have made the same distinctions as before, when we divided herd-maintenance by means of the distinction between creatures with feet and those with wings, and then went on to single out creatures which do not breed with other species and which also lack horns. If we'd made the same series of distinctions in the case of herd-management, we'd have encompassed not only the current variety of kingship, but also kingship as it was in Cronus' time, both within the same formula.

YOUNG SOCRATES: I suppose so. But then what?

VISITOR: It goes without saying that if we'd used this term 'herd-management', we'd never have been faced with the objection that b there is simply no such thing as management, to parallel the earlier, fair objection that there is in human life no art which deserves to be called herd-*maintenance*, and that even if there were, there are plenty of people whose claim to the title is more prominent and valid than that of any kind of king.

YOUNG SOCRATES: Right.

VISITOR: However, when it comes to claiming to have responsibility for managing human society in general – that is, for ruling human beings in all their variety – no art would be in a position to put forward a more prominent or more valid claim than kingship. c

YOUNG SOCRATES: You're right.

VISITOR: Now, the next point for us to appreciate is that we made another serious mistake in the concluding stages.

YOUNG SOCRATES: What?

VISITOR: I'll tell you. Even if we were in fact utterly convinced that there exists a branch of expertise which consists in maintaining two-footed gregarious creatures, we still shouldn't simply have identified it with kingship and statesmanship, as if there were no further work to do.

YOUNG SOCRATES: What should we have done, then?

VISITOR: In the first place, as we've been saying, we should have made up a different name for it – one which related it to manage- d ment rather than maintenance. In the second place, we should then have broken it down, since it isn't the final stage: there are important subsections within it.

YOUNG SOCRATES: What subsections?

31

VISITOR: We might, for instance, have distinguished a divine herdsman from a human manager.

YOUNG SOCRATES: Right.

VISITOR: And once we've singled out management, we have to see what two parts it falls into.

YOUNG SOCRATES: On what basis should we make the division?

VISITOR: It depends on whether it's management by constraint or by consent.

YOUNG SOCRATES: What do you make of this?

e VISITOR: It gives us another perspective from which to see our earlier mistake. We put both the king and the dictator into the same category, which is an extremely silly thing to do, since they not only bear hardly any resemblance to each other in themselves, but the manner of their rule is quite different too.

YOUNG SOCRATES: True.

VISITOR: But we can go back now and correct the error by making the distinction I suggested between management of humans by constraint and by consent.

YOUNG SOCRATES: Yes.

VISITOR: And 'dictatorship' is the term for the management by constraint of unwilling subjects, whereas 'statesmanship' is the term for the management by consent of willing, two-footed, gregarious creatures.[32] So shall we, as our second attempt, propose that a person with this particular kind of managerial expertise is a true statesman-king?

277a YOUNG SOCRATES: Yes, and it looks to me as though this completes our portrait of the statesman.

VISITOR: That would be nice for us, Socrates. But it shouldn't be something just *you* think: I should agree with you as well. In fact, I'm not convinced that our portrait of the king is complete yet. Sculptors sometimes slow down the completion of their work by being too hasty at the wrong time and adding too much material to it, in unnecessarily large quantities, and I think we're behaving like that too. We wanted to show where we went wrong in our

---

[32] The consent of the subjects distinguishes the true king from the dictator or *turannos*, whose rule demands constraint. The reader of the later passage at 296b-e is bound to find trouble rendering it consistent with this one.

first attempt at definition, and to do so not just quickly but impress-ively as well. We thought that the king deserved an impressive illustration from us, so we produced this monstrous myth and felt compelled to find some use for that part of it which was surplus to our requirements. That's why our explanation went on for rather a long time, and in any case we didn't even bring the myth to a conclusion. Our account is exactly like a creature in a painting at the stage when the outline has been completed, but it isn't yet c vivid, and won't be until it has been painted in with the appropriate combination of colours. And yet, provided one has the ability to follow an argument, the spoken word is a far better medium for clarifying any kind of creature than painting and other varieties of manual craft – although they'll do for those who lack this ability.

YOUNG SOCRATES: That's right. But please will you tell me in what respect our account is still incomplete, in your opinion?

VISITOR: It isn't easy to explain large-scale phenomena satisfac- d torily, Socrates, without relying on illustrations. I mean, just when we all seem to have a thorough understanding of something, we wake up, so to speak, to find that it was all a dream, and that in fact we don't understand it at all.

YOUNG SOCRATES: What do you mean?

VISITOR: It seems to me, at the moment, as though the way in which I'm bringing up the topic of how we experience knowledge is very peculiar.

YOUNG SOCRATES: Why?

VISITOR: I find that I need to illustrate illustration itself, my friend!

YOUNG SOCRATES: Why? Don't worry about me, but please tell e us everything.

VISITOR: I'd better explain, then, since you're so eager to listen. You know when children have just started reading ...

YOUNG SOCRATES: What?

VISITOR: They're perfectly clear about all the letters of the alpha-bet as long as they're combined in very short and simple syllables. Under these circumstances, they can tell you correctly which letters are which.[33]

---

[33] The Greek for 'letter', *stoicheion*, also means 'element', and the letters of the alphabet and the ways in which they can be combined into syllables and words provide a ready illustration of the analysis of compounds into more basic elements

278a YOUNG SOCRATES: Of course.

VISITOR: On the other hand, when the letters occur in different combinations, they get confused; their ideas are mistaken and when they try to speak they get things wrong.

YOUNG SOCRATES: True.

VISITOR: Now, there's a very simple and effective way to educate them in what they don't yet know.

YOUNG SOCRATES: What?

VISITOR: First you get them to return to the combinations in which the constituent letters – the same letters – were not causing them difficulties; next, you make them compare these combinations

b with others they still can't recognize; and then you show them that in both cases the combinations have the same features and character. Eventually, you'll have shown them all the cases they get right and compared them with the cases they can't make sense of (which is to use the cases they get right as illustrations), and this will make them capable of identifying any given letter of the alphabet, whatever combination it is a constituent element of, and of recognizing it

c as different from all the rest and also as always the same as itself.

YOUNG SOCRATES: Absolutely.

VISITOR: So it's clear enough now what the point of illustration is, isn't it? It comes about when there's true belief about something, which is the same as something else that occurs in a separate context, and these two things are brought together, and the result is that either of them, and both of them, correctly become the object of a single true judgement.

YOUNG SOCRATES: That sounds right.

VISITOR: We wouldn't be surprised, then, to find that our minds

d tend to work in the same way where the constituents of the universe are concerned, and that in some situations our minds are filled with the certainty of truth about every single constituent, whereas in other situations they are uncertain about everything. And we wouldn't be surprised to find that we sometimes form correct beliefs about the constituents even when they're in combinations, and yet when they're elsewhere, in the long and complex syllables of

of various kinds, as well as for the dependence of our knowledge of compounds on that of their elements. Plato uses the illustration for various purposes in the dialogues; the present one is straightforward, since it is the nature of illustration itself which is being expounded.

the real world, we can make mistakes about these same constituents.

YOUNG SOCRATES: No, that wouldn't be at all surprising.

VISITOR: Because it's impossible for false belief to act as a basis from which to progress to even the tiniest sliver of truth and so e acquire knowledge.[34]

YOUNG SOCRATES: Yes, that's more or less impossible.

VISITOR: So if this is how things are, then you and I won't cause offence if we first try to understand the nature of the issue as a whole by examining a small and particular illustration of it, and then change tack and transfer our attention from lesser cases to the most important issue of all – kingship – and try this time to use an illustration to gain expert knowledge of the art of tending to a state. Then we'll have changed our dream into conscious awareness.

YOUNG SOCRATES: Yes, I'm sure we're on the right track.

VISITOR: We'd better resume our interrupted discussion, then, 279a so that we can exclude all those thousands of people who dispute the king's claim to responsibility for states, and so leave the king alone in place; and we were saying that an illustration would help us in this task.

YOUNG SOCRATES: Yes.

VISITOR: To act as an illustration, then, we need something which involves the same activity as statesmanship, but which is very accessible, so that we can use it as a point of comparison to help us discover to our satisfaction what we're looking for. What could we use? I tell you what, Socrates: if nothing else strikes us as b obviously suitable, why don't we take weaving? Perhaps not the whole of weaving, though: weaving in wool will probably be enough. If we take even just this aspect of weaving, I think it will give us the information we want.[35]

---

[34] Reading πῶς γάρ with the MSS.

[35] The definition of weaving is (i) an illustration of the kind of definition of the statesman which it is the ostensible purpose of the dialogue to achieve; the relatively trivial nature of the illustration is itself a lesson in not despising the obvious and the help it can give with the less obvious; (ii) an illustration of what the statesman actually does; at 305e ff. the statesman's task in producing a unified community is itself lengthily described as a kind of weaving. There is no warning here of application (ii), which indeed turns weaving, described here in the most literal possible way (this passage is our major source for the detail of ancient weaving) into a metaphor, and arguably pushes it further than it can go. Plato is apt to overload his illustrations and imagery, risking confusion in the reader.

YOUNG SOCRATES: Yes, I don't see why it shouldn't.

VISITOR: All right. Now, previously we distinguished all the various subsections by dividing them one after another, so why don't

c we do the same for weaving? Why don't we race as swiftly as possible through the whole lot so that we can quickly get back to the main point?

YOUNG SOCRATES: What do you mean?

VISITOR: The best answer I can give to that is actually to go through it all.

YOUNG SOCRATES: That's an excellent idea.

VISITOR: Well, all manufactured items and possessions serve one of two purposes: they either do something or they protect against something being done. Protection is achieved either by antidotes

d (supernatural or human) or by defences. Defences are either military equipment or barriers. Barriers are either screens or buffers against heat and cold. These buffers are either shelters or coverings. Coverings are either things we put under our bodies or things we put on our bodies. Things we put on our bodies are either cut from a single piece of material or are composite. The composite ones are either stitched together or joined without the use of

e stitching. The unstitched ones are either made out of the fibres of plants or from animal hair. Those made from animal hair are either cemented together by glues made out of liquids and solids or are joined together by linking strands of the same material. It is these manufactured protective coverings, joined together out of a single material, to which we give the name 'cloaks'. And why don't we derive a name from the product and call the art which

280a is particularly responsible for cloaks 'cloak-making'? That would fit in with our earlier idea that statesmanship is the art which is responsible for managing a state. And what about adding that weaving – or at least the far from insubstantial part of it which is concerned with the production of cloaks – differs only in name from this 'cloak-making' of ours, just as in the other sphere we concluded earlier that kingship differs only in name from statesmanship?

YOUNG SOCRATES: There's nothing wrong with doing that.

VISITOR: Now, we ought next to think the matter through and

b see that if our account of the weaving of cloaks were taken to be definitive, which might well happen, this would be due to an inability to appreciate that although the weaving of cloaks has been distinguished from a lot of related processes, there are others, closely associated with it, from which it has not yet been separated.

YOUNG SOCRATES: What related processes has it been distinguished from?

VISITOR: It looks as though you haven't understood what I've been saying. Perhaps I'd better go back over it. I'll start at the end, because I'm sure you'll see the connection between the weaving of cloaks and an art we divided off from it a moment ago – I mean rug-making, which we eliminated by means of the distinction between putting things on our bodies and putting things under our bodies.

YOUNG SOCRATES: Yes, I see.

VISITOR: And we also excluded the whole field of making items c out of flax and broom and in general the fibres of plants, as we not unreasonably called them a short while ago. Then again, we separated off felting and any manufacturing process which employs sewing and stitching – which is to say, above all, shoe-making.

YOUNG SOCRATES: Yes.

VISITOR: Then within the area of expertise which deals with coverings cut from a single piece of material, we eliminated expertise at working with skins, and we also excluded techniques which deal with shelters – which is to say all the procedures used in house-building and in the construction industry in general which afford protection against water, and all those which supply us with barriers whose job is to inhibit theft and acts of violence (the manufacture d of lids, for instance, and door-hanging), which are considered to be aspects of carpentry. We excluded the manufacture of armour as well, which is a subsection of the important and many-faceted sphere of manufacturing defences. And right at the beginning we also excluded the whole domain of sorcery, in so far as it is e concerned with antidotes. And so we were apparently left with exactly the art we'd been looking for – one which affords protection against cold weather by manufacturing defence in wool, and which goes by the name of weaving.

YOUNG SOCRATES: Yes, that seems reasonable.

VISITOR: But in fact, Socrates, our account is still incomplete, because the very first task in the manufacture of cloaks seems to do the opposite of weaving. 281a

YOUNG SOCRATES: What do you mean?

VISITOR: Well, to weave is to combine, isn't it?

YOUNG SOCRATES: Yes.

VISITOR: Whereas the task I'm thinking of disassembles and disentangles things.

YOUNG SOCRATES: But what task is it?

VISITOR: It's carding. I mean, we wouldn't want to call carding weaving or a carder a weaver, would we?

YOUNG SOCRATES: Certainly not.

VISITOR: And that's not all. It would be odd – false, even – to use the name 'weaving' for the production of the threads which
b go to make up the warp and the weft.

YOUNG SOCRATES: Of course it would.

VISITOR: Then there are fulling and darning, with all their aspects. Should we deny that in some sense they're responsible for and tend to clothing? Or, if we don't deny it, should we describe all of them too as weaving?

YOUNG SOCRATES: No, not at all.

VISITOR: But all the branches of expertise I've mentioned will dispute the claim of weaving to tend to and make clothing; they'll grant that weaving has a crucial role to play, but they'll assign themselves important parts as well.
c YOUNG SOCRATES: Yes.

VISITOR: And it won't stop with them either. The crafts which manufacture the tools which enable weaving to achieve its results are bound to claim to be responsible as well, in a subordinate fashion, for every woven item, don't you think?

YOUNG SOCRATES: You're quite right.

VISITOR: So suppose we say that of all the processes which are responsible for woollen clothing, there is none which has a finer or more important part to play than weaving. Is that account of weaving – or rather, of the aspect of weaving we chose – definite
d enough? Wouldn't it be better for us to say that it is true, but will remain vague and incomplete until we've distinguished weaving from all those other processes?

YOUNG SOCRATES: That's right.

VISITOR: The logical next step, then, is for our actions to suit these words of ours. Yes?

YOUNG SOCRATES: Of course.

VISITOR: The first point for us to notice is that there are two areas of expertise involved in any and every activity.

YOUNG SOCRATES: What are they?

VISITOR: One is subordinately responsible for things happening, the other is directly responsible.

YOUNG SOCRATES: What do you mean?

VISITOR: All the processes which don't actually make the item, e but supply the ones which do with their equipment (without which none of these branches of expertise could possibly carry out its prescribed job) have subordinate responsibility for the item, whereas those which create the actual item are directly responsible for it.

YOUNG SOCRATES: That makes sense.

VISITOR: So should our next step be to claim that the crafts which manufacture spindles and shuttles and all the other implements which are involved in the making of clothing are all subordinately responsible for it, whereas those which tend to and manufacture the actual clothing are directly responsible for it?

YOUNG SOCRATES: There's nothing wrong with that.

VISITOR: Now, among those which are directly responsible for 282a clothing, it seems perfectly reasonable to take washing, darning and all the processes which tend to clothing in this sense (and which are all aspects of the extensive art of ornamentation) and to encompass the subsection of ornamentation that we find here by describing them as all constituting 'fulling'.

YOUNG SOCRATES: Fine.

VISITOR: However, carding and spinning and all the other aspects of the actual manufacture of clothing of the type we're talking about constitute a single area of expertise which is universally recognized, namely wool-working.

YOUNG SOCRATES: Of course.

VISITOR: Now, wool-working has two subsections, we may say, b each of which is an aspect of two areas of expertise at the same time.

YOUNG SOCRATES: What do you mean?

VISITOR: Let's take carding, along with half of the use to which the shuttle is put and everything else which takes apart material which had been forming a compound whole. We could surely describe them as constituting one subsection of wool-working. Now, we also found that there are a pair of important techniques which apply to everything we do, namely combination and separation.

YOUNG SOCRATES: Yes.

VISITOR: Well, everything I just mentioned, including carding,
c belongs to the category of separation, since, whatever they're called, they are simply processes of separating either untreated wool or threads, although different methods are involved depending on whether one is using a shuttle or one's bare hands.

YOUNG SOCRATES: That's right.

VISITOR: On the other hand, there's also an aspect of wool-working which belongs to the category of combination as well as to wool-working. We should take this aspect into consideration too, by ignoring all the processes of separation which we found within wool-working. Then we've divided wool-working into two halves, one which involves separation and one which involves combination.

YOUNG SOCRATES: I'm happy with that division.

VISITOR: Now, we're going to have to subdivide the section which
d is simultaneously an aspect of combination and an aspect of wool-working, Socrates, if we're to gain a firm enough grip on our intended quarry, weaving.

YOUNG SOCRATES: In that case, we'd better make this further subdivision.

VISITOR: Yes, and I think we should make it as follows: one part involves winding, while the other part involves interlacing.

YOUNG SOCRATES: I wonder if I've understood your point. I take you to mean that the preparation of the threads of the warp involves winding.

VISITOR: Yes, but not just the warp: the preparation of the weft does as well. Can you think of a method of making the weft which doesn't involve winding?

YOUNG SOCRATES: No.

e VISITOR: I want you now to make distinctions within both winding and interlacing. I expect you'll find the distinctions relevant.

YOUNG SOCRATES: How?

VISITOR: You'll see. When a piece of carded wool has been stretched out and flattened, it's called a 'strip', isn't it?

YOUNG SOCRATES: Yes.

VISITOR: And when this strip has been wound by a spindle and has become yarn, any solid yarn is called 'warp' and the process of directing the yarn is called 'warp-spinning'.

YOUNG SOCRATES: That's right.

VISITOR: On the other hand, all the yarn which is not so compact after it has been wound into threads, and which is soft enough to be interlaced with the warp when pressure is exerted on it in the dressing process, is known as the 'weft', and the process of getting it to do what it's supposed to do is called 'weft-spinning'.   283a

YOUNG SOCRATES: True.

VISITOR: The aspect of weaving which we're after is now in full view. When that subdivision of the process of combination which wool-working involves creates a tight fabric by interlacing weft and warp, the resulting fabric as a whole is called a woollen garment, and the art which is responsible for this is called weaving.

YOUNG SOCRATES: You're quite right.

VISITOR: All right. Now, why on earth didn't we define weaving   b straight away as the process of interlacing weft and warp? Why did we go about it in such a roundabout way, which entailed defining all kinds of other things, when there was no point?

YOUNG SOCRATES: *I* don't think anything that's been said has been pointless.

VISITOR: There's no good reason why you *should* think it pointless, Socrates,[36] but you might at some time in the future, and I want to guard against the possibility – the very real possibility – of your contracting that kind of sickness. So I'd like to offer some remarks which bear upon cases like this one.   c

YOUNG SOCRATES: Please do.

VISITOR: I think we should start by considering excess and deficiency in general. Only then can we ever sensibly either approve or disapprove of unwarranted length and brevity in discussions like ours.

YOUNG SOCRATES: That's a good idea.

VISITOR: Well, the correct way to proceed, to my mind, would be to think about these things in themselves, out of any context.

---

[36] Retaining καὶ θαυμαστόν γε οὐδέν with the MSS.

YOUNG SOCRATES: Which things?

VISITOR: Length and brevity, and excess[37] and deficiency in gen-
d eral – which is to say, all the things with which measurement deals.

YOUNG SOCRATES: Yes.

VISITOR: Now, let's divide measurement into two parts. Our present concerns will get nowhere unless we do.

YOUNG SOCRATES: Could you explain how to make the division?

VISITOR: Yes. The division takes account, on the one hand, of
the fact that things are large and small relative to one another,
and on the other hand of the fact that there does exist something
which is a necessary prerequisite for qualities to occur.

YOUNG SOCRATES: What do you mean?

VISITOR: Don't you think it's inevitable that something which is
larger can only be larger than something which is smaller, and
conversely that something which is smaller can only be smaller
e than something which is larger?

YOUNG SOCRATES: Yes, I do.

VISITOR: But what about exceeding and falling short of due
measure? Don't you think this is also a real feature of the things
people say, and of the things they do too? And doesn't it in fact
provide us with our chief criterion for distinguishing good and bad
people?[38]

YOUNG SOCRATES: Yes, I suppose it does.

VISITOR: So we'd better claim that there are *two* ways in which
things can be, and can be assessed as, large and small. A short
while ago we were tending to assume that things are only to be
assessed relative to one another, but that was wrong. What we're
saying now is an improvement, and we'd better acknowledge that
things can be assessed not only relative to one another, but also
relative to due measure. Shall I tell you why this distinction is
important?

YOUNG SOCRATES: Yes, please.

---

[37] There is no reason not to retain ὑπερβολῆς with the MSS.

[38] The introduction of the *metrion* or due measure between excess and falling short
is abrupt, as is the claim that this is an intuitive way of distinguishing good from
bad people. We have no way of assessing Plato's claim here. Aristotle does not
claim that his own theory of the 'mean' (*meson*) between excess and falling short
is particularly intuitive, though he makes it basic to his account of virtue. Perhaps
Plato here assumes that what he says will be taken as an application of the common
saying 'nothing in excess' (*mēden agan*).

VISITOR: If one holds that, in the nature of things, an object can 284a
only be called 'larger' in relation to something smaller, then there's
no such thing as a criterion of due measure, is there?
YOUNG SOCRATES: No.
VISITOR: Well, wouldn't this position get rid of expertise and its
products altogether? Wouldn't it do away with statesmanship, which
is the object of our enquiry, and weaving, which we've just been
talking about? The point is that all branches of knowledge are very
careful to avoid exceeding and falling short of due measure, as
you know; they don't regard it as something which doesn't exist,
but as something which creates difficulties for them in their work.
In fact, any excellence and beauty their products have are due b
precisely to the fact that they *don't* do away with due measure.
YOUNG SOCRATES: Of course.
VISITOR: Well, if we do away with statesmanship, our enquiry
into the branch of knowledge which constitutes kingship will be
unable to proceed any further, won't it?
YOUNG SOCRATES: Definitely.
VISITOR: Now, in the *Sophist* there was a point when we insisted
that something which 'is not' still 'is', because this was the issue
which had made us lose our grip on the argument. Should we do
the same now as well? Should we simply insist that 'more' and
'less' are to be assessed not only against each other, but also against
the phenomenon of due measure? The point is that if we don't c
agree on this, we'll never able to come up with an unassailable
argument that a statesman or anyone else who works in the real
world is in possession of a branch of knowledge.[39]
YOUNG SOCRATES: Then I'm sure we should do the same now
as well.
VISITOR: We're letting ourselves in for even more work than we
did before, Socrates – and you know how much time we've already
taken! But there's an assumption we'd be perfectly justified in
making about this matter.

---

[39] The existence of due measure is necessary for expertise to exist, and if there is
no such thing then the search for an account of the statesman is futile. However,
it is odd for Plato to compare this point with the point about being and not-being
in the *Sophist*, which is established differently, as the conclusion of an argument
(see *Sophist* 258b–259c). Further, he goes on to claim that the existence of expertise
and the existence of due measure are mutually entailing, making it unclear why

YOUNG SOCRATES: What?

d VISITOR: That when one day we come to demonstrate what absolute precision is, we'll need the principle we've just stated. However, we're currently engaged on a demonstration that is perfectly adequate for our present purpose, and I think it's going to help us enormously to have agreed that the two notions go hand in hand – that the various branches of knowledge do exist, and also that 'greater' and 'less' are to be assessed against the phenomenon of due measure as well as against each other. Without due measure there is no such thing as expertise, and without expertise there is no such thing as due measure. The non-existence of either of them results in the non-existence of the other.

e YOUNG SOCRATES: You're right. But then what?

VISITOR: The next step is obviously for us to fulfil our earlier promise and divide measurement in two, as follows. We'll make one section consist of all the branches of expertise which assess quantity, length, depth, breadth and speed against an opposite value, while the other section will consist of all the branches of expertise which assess things against due measure, suitability, timeliness, desirability and so on – qualities which are located in the mean rather than the extremes.[40]

YOUNG SOCRATES: Yes, the two sections you've mentioned are clearly different from each other. They're pretty wide-ranging, too.

VISITOR: Yes, and you know how all those intellectuals try to 285a make a clever point, Socrates,[41] by claiming from time to time that there's nothing which can't be measured – this is in fact exactly what we're saying now. In some way or another, everything which takes skill employs measurement. However, because people aren't familiar with the method of enquiry which involves dividing things into their separate categories, they overlook the huge differences between things, lump them all together without pause for thought, and treat them as all more or less the same. Alternatively, they make the opposite mistake: they divide things up, but not into

the point about due measure is supposed to give independent support to the point about expertise.

[40] 'Mean' (*meson*) is used in Aristotle's way, as the point that is appropriate or due between extremes of excess and defect.

[41] The 'intellectuals' here may be Pythagoreans, but the reference is unclear. Cf. the passage about kinds of knowledge and the role of measurement and mathematics at *Philebus* 55d ff.

subsections. The proper procedure is as follows. Suppose you notice in a preliminary fashion that a large number of objects share b some feature or other; you should carry on until you've seen all the differences within that shared feature which form distinct categories. And if, on the other hand, it's the enormous diversity within the profusion of things that has caught your attention, you shouldn't let yourself be put off by this and stop before you've gathered all their common qualities together within the enclosure of a single shared feature and clothed them in the reality of a given category.[42]

Anyway, so much for that, and I think we've said enough about excess and deficiency as well. The thing to fix in our minds is our discovery that there are two ways of measuring excess and c deficiency; we should remember what we said they were.

YOUNG SOCRATES: We will.

VISITOR: The next point which greets us is relevant not just to our immediate concerns but to the whole business of rational enquiry.

YOUNG SOCRATES: What is it?

VISITOR: Here's a question we might be asked about students learning at school: 'When a student is asked to spell some word or other, is the point of the test the particular word the student d has been set, or is it for him to become better at spelling any word he's ever set?'

YOUNG SOCRATES: The point is obviously the student's general literacy.

VISITOR: And what about our quest for the statesman? Is the point of it just the particular task at hand, or is it for us to become better dialecticians generally?[43]

YOUNG SOCRATES: Again, the point is obviously general.

VISITOR: Yes, I'm sure that no one in his right mind would want to make an account of weaving his goal just for its own sake! But

---

[42] This returns to the point that philosophical enquiry should result in understanding of things that form objective natural unities, even where this is not obvious at first sight (cf. *Philebus* 16c–17e); to reach these natural unities we may have to do a lot of hard and strange work (as in the account in the *Statesman* itself).

[43] It need not be, as sometimes thought, that the point of the dialogue is to develop a topic-neutral ability that could just as well have been practised on something else. Rather, getting an adequate account of the expertise of ruling is not philosophically self-contained: in deepening our understanding of one area of philosophy we thereby improve the philosophical skills that will also be employed elsewhere.

I think most people overlook the fact that only *some* things are so
e constituted as to have perceptible likenesses which are easily
grasped; in these cases, when you're asked for an account of
something, you can respond simply by showing the corresponding
likeness – it's no bother and it doesn't even require you to say
anything. However, there are other things – things of the utmost
286a significance and importance – for which there is no artefact which,
used as a likeness, would automatically give people the right
impression so that, if you wanted to satisfy a questioner's mind,
you could adequately do so simply by showing the object in a way
which suited one of the questioner's senses. And that's why we
have to practise until we're capable of giving and following a verbal
account of things. You see, the most valuable and important things
are incorporeal, and the *only* way to give a clear impression of
them is by means of a verbal account. And they are the point of
our whole discussion. But it's always easier to practise on things
b of lesser importance, rather than on the more crucial things.[44]

YOUNG SOCRATES: You're perfectly right.

VISITOR: I think we should bear in mind why we raised this
whole topic.

YOUNG SOCRATES: Why did we?

VISITOR: The main reason was the dissatisfaction we expressed
about the length at which we'd discussed weaving, the unwinding
of the universe and, in the case of the sophist, how something
which 'is not' still 'is'. We were wondering whether we'd gone on
too long, and we were cross with ourselves because we were
c afraid that, in all these cases, we'd padded the discussion out with
unnecessary material. I want you to appreciate, then, that the reason
we raised all the points we were talking about before was so that
we would never again feel worried on this score.

YOUNG SOCRATES: I'll see to it. Please go on.

VISITOR: All right. The point is that before you and I criticize
or acclaim any of our discussions for being short or long, we

---

[44] Plato repeats his insistence that the understanding we get from using our intellects
has more worthwhile results than what we can get from studying the world
empirically. Presumably he thinks the reminder timely because of all the attention
that has been paid to highly empirical matters such as weaving and the like as
material for the intellectual process in question. What he has in mind primarily,
of course, are the objectively unified forms or categories that philosophical discussion and analysis discover.

should remember what we've just been saying. We shouldn't judge how long a discussion is by comparing its length with that of another discussion; we should use the kind of measurement we were trying to fix in our minds earlier, and assess it according to d its suitability.

YOUNG SOCRATES: Right.

VISITOR: Now, even suitability isn't a standard we should use indiscriminately. For instance, there's a length which is appropriate for giving pleasure, but we won't take the slightest interest in that. Or again, there's the criterion of resolving the task before us as easily and as quickly as possible, but what we've been saying suggests that, although this should be welcomed, it is of secondary rather than primary importance. No, by far the most important thing for us to value is competence at this method of division into categories. It also suggests that even an extremely long discussion e is worthwhile – that its length is nothing to get upset about – as long as it increases the ability of the audience to discover the truth, and that the same goes for discussions which are rather short as well. And that's not all. Another implication is that anyone who criticizes these kinds of discussions for their length and complains at the circuitous routes they take should not lightly and over-hastily dismiss them by merely criticizing the length of the discussion; he 287a should realize that he also has to prove that a shorter discussion would have been more effective at increasing the participants' competence at dialectic and would have made them better at discovering arguments which clearly display the truth; and he needn't worry in the slightest whether others, using different criteria, think badly or well of a discussion – he can even pretend not to have heard their comments at all.[45]

Anyway, I think that's enough on this topic. Do you agree? Let's return to the statesman and see what effect our illustration from b weaving has on him.

YOUNG SOCRATES: That's a good idea. Let's do that.

[45] Readers have been understandably dismayed by the way in which Plato makes the visitor comment on the apparent length and irrelevance of his digressions in a way which is itself lengthy and not obviously relevant. It is best to take this passage at face value: Plato is aware that the new way of doing philosophy visible in the *Statesman* will seem to many to be boring and irrelevant after the exciting treatment in, say, the *Republic*, and he is underlining the claim that philosophy requires more careful and pedestrian procedures than we find in that work.

VISITOR: Well, we've been fairly thorough in distinguishing kingship from its rivals, especially all those which are concerned with maintaining herds. We're left, I think, with procedures which have direct or subordinate responsibility for the actual state, and we'd better start by making distinctions among them.

YOUNG SOCRATES: Right.

VISITOR: Do you appreciate how hard it is to divide them into
c two? I think you'll find it easier to see why as we go on.

YOUNG SOCRATES: That's what we'd better do, then.

VISITOR: If we can't divide them into two, then let's treat them like a sacrificial carcass and carve them at their joints, because we have to produce as few subsections as possible, whatever we're dividing.[46]

YOUNG SOCRATES: How shall we proceed in the present case?

VISITOR: The same way as we did before. Earlier, as I'm sure you remember, we counted all the professions which supplied equipment in the field of weaving as having subordinate responsibility.

YOUNG SOCRATES: Yes.

VISITOR: We'd better do exactly the same now, then; it's even
d more important this time. We must classify all the professions which manufacture some major or minor implement for society as having subordinate responsibility for the state. These implements may be indispensable for the state, and therefore for statesmanship, but on the other hand we won't count any of them as products of kingship.

YOUNG SOCRATES: No, that's right.

VISITOR: Now, we've taken on a difficult job here. It isn't easy to distinguish this subordinate class from everything else, because it seems perfectly plausible to say of *anything* that it is a piece of
e equipment for *something*. Still, not all property in a state falls into this class – there's another kind as well, don't you think?

YOUNG SOCRATES: What?

VISITOR: The kind of things which have a different function, in the sense that the reason they're made is not to produce results, but to look after something once it has been made.

---

[46] Here it is made explicit that the point of division is to analyse the subject-matter to find the natural objective categories, and that a method like dividing into two has value only as a means towards this end, not intrinsically.

YOUNG SOCRATES: What are you talking about?

VISITOR: There are a great many different varieties of this kind of object. Some of them are made for dry goods, some for liquids, some are fire-resistant, some aren't; but, when given a single label, they're all called 'containers'. It's a category with a lot of members, and I don't think it has any connection at all with the branch of knowledge we're trying to track down. 288a

YOUNG SOCRATES: Of course it doesn't.

VISITOR: Now, we'd better appreciate that, apart from these two classes, there's a third one, which is again a very large class. Some of its members go on land, some on water; some are mobile, some stationary; some are remarkable, some ordinary; but they all have a single name because they all have the purpose of being sat on, of being a seat for something or someone.

YOUNG SOCRATES: And what kind of object is this?

VISITOR: It's usually called a 'support'. Now, it's not really the job of statesmanship to work with supports: carpentry, pottery and metal-work are more relevant in that context.

YOUNG SOCRATES: I see what you mean.

VISITOR: What about this as a fourth subsection? Take the b majority of the items we were talking about a while back – clothing in general, most armour, all walls and fortifications of earth and stone, and so on and so forth. Don't you think we should find a distinct class here? Since the reason all these things are made is for defence, we could hardly go wrong if we called the whole category 'defences' – and it would be considerably closer to the truth to say that building and weaving, rather than statesmanship, are basically responsible for working with them.

YOUNG SOCRATES: Yes.

VISITOR: And what about ornamentation and painting and the c representational works of art which painters and musicians produce? Shall we count them as a fifth subsection? Their *raison d'être* is pleasure, and there's a single term which accurately describes them.

YOUNG SOCRATES: What?

VISITOR: Well, you know the term 'amusement' . . .

YOUNG SOCRATES: What of it?

VISITOR: It makes a good single term for all the things I mentioned, because none of them serves an important purpose: they're all done just for fun.

d YOUNG SOCRATES: Yes, again I'm pretty sure I see what you mean.

VISITOR: Now, there is also the business of supplying the members of all these subsections with the materials out of which or in which all the branches of expertise we've mentioned manufacture their products. It constitutes a many-faceted class, consisting of things which owe their existence to a large number of areas of expertise other than ones we've already mentioned. Shall we count it as a sixth subsection?

YOUNG SOCRATES: I'm not clear what you're talking about.

VISITOR: I mean gold and silver and mined material as a whole; I mean all the material which wood-work and wicker-work gains from trees being felled and things in general being cut down; I also mean all the various processes like stripping plants of their
e outer layers and skinning animals (which is to say leather-working); and I mean the production of cork and papyrus and bindings – processes which turn elementary materials into composite manufactured items. We can refer to this category as a whole as 'primordial and elementary human property', and it is definitely not the job of kingship to work with it.

YOUNG SOCRATES: That's right.

VISITOR: Then there's the acquisition of food and other substances which have the capacity of tending to the body when their particles are mixed with those of the body. We'd better have this
289a as a seventh subsection and, for want of a better term, I suggest we refer to it as a whole as 'nourishment'. However, it would be more realistic of us to count it as falling within the province of agriculture, hunting, exercising, medicine or cookery rather than that of statesmanship.

YOUNG SOCRATES: Of course it would.

VISITOR: Well, it seems to me that we've given a thorough description of the phenomenon and that our seven subsections include every kind of property, except perhaps domestic animals. Here's the list: there's the primordial category (which we should
b probably have put first), then implements, containers, supports, defences, amusements and nutriments. Anything we haven't mentioned – and I don't think we've overlooked anything important –

can fit into one of our seven categories. Consider coins, for instance, and signet-rings and seals in general. In themselves, they don't form a single broad category to rival the others: it might in some cases be artificial, but they can somehow or other be made to belong with 'ornamentation', perhaps, or with 'implements'. As for the kind of property which consists of domesticated living creatures (I'm not counting slaves here), you'll find that our earlier c category, 'herd-maintenance', can accommodate them all.

YOUNG SOCRATES: I agree.

VISITOR: We're left, then, with slaves and assistants in general. My guess is that we'll find those who dispute the king's claim to be responsible for the actual fabric of the state somewhere among them, which would parallel our earlier suggestion that the weaver's rivals are those who are concerned with spinning and carding and so on. Everyone else has only subordinate responsibility, as we put it, and the argument we've just concluded has eliminated them: the sphere of operation of the statesman-king is quite different from *their* work. d

YOUNG SOCRATES: Yes, that does seem to be so.

VISITOR: All right, then. Let's try to get a really good look at the ones we're left with, by inspecting them at close quarters.

YOUNG SOCRATES: That's a good idea.

VISITOR: Now, it's clear that the way of life and the experiences of the most obvious assistants – most obvious from our present perspective – fail to confirm our guess.

YOUNG SOCRATES: Who do you mean?

VISITOR: People who've been bought and are consequently pieces of property. No one could possibly dispute our assertion that they e have the status of slaves – or that they have no claim at all to kingship.

YOUNG SOCRATES: Of course not.

VISITOR: What about all those free men who choose to take on the job of assisting the artisans we were talking about a short while ago, by distributing on a quid pro quo basis agricultural produce and the things the other artisans make? Some have stalls in the market-place, others go from state to state by land and sea; they exchange money for goods, or money for money, and we call them money-changers, traders, merchant shippers, and retailers. Do they have any kind of 290a claim to statesmanship?

YOUNG SOCRATES: Some of those who are involved with commerce might, I suppose.

VISITOR: But when we're faced with people who work for money and who don't hesitate to assist anyone at all who wants to hire them, surely it's quite impossible for us to think that they are entitled to kingship?[47]

YOUNG SOCRATES: Of course it is.

VISITOR: Then there are other forms of service. What are we to think about people who spend their time on them?

YOUNG SOCRATES: What forms of service? Who do you mean?

b VISITOR: Heralds, for instance, and other experts at some governmental task or other – like those people whose assistance has so often been sought that they've become skilled scribes. What are we to think about them?

YOUNG SOCRATES: You said it yourself just now – they're assistants, not actual rulers of states.

VISITOR: But I'm sure I wasn't just imagining things when I said that we'd find the statesman's arch-rivals here, despite the fact that it does seem extremely strange to be looking for his rivals in the

c domain of service.

YOUNG SOCRATES: Yes, it certainly does.

VISITOR: So let's get to even closer grips with the assistants we haven't yet examined. There are those who know how to perform services in the field of divination, because they're supposed to be able to interpret the gods for people.

YOUNG SOCRATES: Yes.

VISITOR: And then there are priests in general, who are traditionally regarded as knowing how to offer the gifts we give the gods in our

d sacrifices in a manner which will be acceptable to them, and how to use prayer to ask them for good things to come our way – both of these functions being aspects of service.

YOUNG SOCRATES: Yes, I suppose so.

VISITOR: Well, now I think we're dealing with at least our quarry's tracks, so to speak, in the sense that priests and diviners have a

---

[47] The visitor has distinguished the possessor of the statesman's expertise from the producers of various products and now from people who are engaged in productive labour. The whole of what we would call the economic side of political life is thus regarded as mere material for the ruler's skill to work on, and for Plato it does not even have any obvious distinction from the non-productive skills which follow.

thoroughly dignified image, and the work they do is so important that they've acquired a high-powered reputation. In fact, in Egypt a king isn't allowed to rule unless he's also a priest; even if he had previously belonged to another caste and had become king by force, he has to be initiated after the event into the priestly caste. It's also noticeable that in many Greek states the most important religious rituals have been made the responsibility of the most important governmental offices. There's a particularly clear example of this phenomenon here in Athens: I hear that the most solemn of the traditional sacrifices on behalf of the whole state have been assigned to the person who is elected 'king'.

YOUNG SOCRATES: That's true.

VISITOR: We'd better see what we can find out about these lottery-elected kings,[48] then, and priests as well, and their assistants – and there's another huge crowd of people who have just become recognizable, now that we've distinguished these various categories of assistant.[49]

YOUNG SOCRATES: Who do you mean?

VISITOR: They're a very peculiar lot.

YOUNG SOCRATES: Why?

VISITOR: They form a motley band, or at least that's the impression I got when I had a look at them a moment ago. Quite a few of them look like lions, centaurs and creatures like that; a great many look like satyrs and those beasts which are weak and cunning and can rapidly take on each others' looks and abilities. Ah! I think I've just recognized who they are, Socrates.

YOUNG SOCRATES: I can't wait to hear what you have to say, because it looks as though you've seen an oddity.

VISITOR: Yes, I have – in the sense that describing something as odd is always the result of ignorance, and that sums up my own condition at the moment. When I saw the gang of people who are involved in state politics, I was suddenly confused.

YOUNG SOCRATES: Who are they?

VISITOR: They include the person who is the supreme illusionist, the most skilled sophist of them all. It won't be at all easy, but we're

291a

b

c

---

[48] One of the Athenian state officials held the title of 'king' and fulfilled religious duties originally carried out by real kings. The visitor points to the irony of the title of king belonging to an office which was filled, as were most offices under the democracy, by selection by lottery, a procedure obviously blind to merit.

[49] Retaining νῦν with MSS. BW.

going to have to differentiate him from the true statesman-king, otherwise we won't be certain that what we're seeing really is the one we're after.

YOUNG SOCRATES: And we should never relax our efforts to find *him*.

VISITOR: No, I quite agree. But here's a question for you.

YOUNG SOCRATES: What?

d VISITOR: There's a form of government which is monarchy, isn't there?

YOUNG SOCRATES: Yes.

VISITOR: And I suppose one could say that the next form of government is when power is in the hands of the few.

YOUNG SOCRATES: Of course.

VISITOR: A third type of political system is the rule of the many, which is known as democracy. Yes?

YOUNG SOCRATES: Certainly.

VISITOR: Now aren't these three systems of government in a sense five? Don't two of them give rise to other systems as well, with different names?

YOUNG SOCRATES: Which other systems are you thinking of?

e VISITOR: If we now take into consideration whether they involve constraint or consent, poverty or wealth, and regard or disregard for law, we have a criterion for dividing each of the two systems into two parts.[50] Let's take monarchy first. Since it appears in two different guises, there are two terms for it – dictatorship and kingship.

YOUNG SOCRATES: Naturally.

VISITOR: And a state which is controlled by a few of its members may be called either an aristocracy or an oligarchy.

YOUNG SOCRATES: Yes.

VISITOR: As for democracy, it doesn't make any difference whether
292a the general populace rules over the propertied class by constraint or

[50] Plato's way of dividing up forms of government relies on commonsensical criteria, and marks a sharp break from *Republic* books 8 and 9, where types of government are described in terms driven by the analogy of soul and state, so that Plato describes, for example, the oligarchic person and the oligarchic state, the democratic person and the democratic state, and so on. Without this analogy Plato here classifies forms of government in a way which influenced Aristotle (see *Politics* 1279a22–1280a6 and 1289a26–b26, of which the second passage seems clearly to refer to this one). Aristotle's division is simpler: he classifies each of the kinds one/few/many rulers by whether or not it is governed in the common interest, or in the interest solely of the rulers themselves.

by consent: people still invariably tend to use the same term for it.[51]

YOUNG SOCRATES: True.

VISITOR: Now, the principles which distinguish each of these political systems are, for instance, whether power is in the hands of one person or a few people or many people, whether the ruling class is rich or poor, whether rule is by constraint or consent, and whether or not the system happens to involve a written legal code. Doesn't this exclude them from being perfect systems?

YOUNG SOCRATES: Why should it?

VISITOR: You need to consider the matter more carefully. Try to b follow my line of reasoning.

YOUNG SOCRATES: Go on.

VISITOR: There's something we said right at the beginning of our discussion. Shall we continue to affirm it, or do we disagree with it now?

YOUNG SOCRATES: What are you referring to?

VISITOR: We said that government by a king was a branch of knowledge, didn't we?

YOUNG SOCRATES: Yes.

VISITOR: And we were more precise than that. We narrowed the branches of knowledge that interested us down to an evaluative kind and an instructional kind.

YOUNG SOCRATES: Yes.

VISITOR: And we broke the instructional kind down into a branch that is responsible for inanimate things and a branch that is responsible for living creatures. The process of continually making these c kinds of divisions has brought us to where we are now, but we've borne in mind throughout that kingship is a sort of knowledge – even if we haven't been able to specify with enough precision exactly what sort.

YOUNG SOCRATES: That's an accurate summary.

VISITOR: What I want us to appreciate, then, is that if we're to be consistent with these early stages of the argument, the standard by

[51] Greek usage does not in fact support this view. The terms seem to be used in a vaguer and more evaluative way, supporters of the rule of the few calling it aristocracy and opponents oligarchy, for example. Derogatory terms for the rule of the many emerge only later (for example 'ochlocracy' or rule of the mob, in Polybius). Aristotle, who uses 'democracy' only for what he considers the deviated form of the rule of the many (rule in the interests of the rulers, not of all) is forced to bring in a new and unintuitive term, *politeia*, for the good form.

which we assess constitutions should not be the number of its rulers, consent and constraint, poverty and wealth; it should be a branch of knowledge.

d YOUNG SOCRATES: But we must of course be consistent.

VISITOR: It inevitably follows, then, that what we have to try to find out is which of these systems of government in fact possesses knowledge of what is probably the most difficult, and the most important, kind of rulership to master – ruling over human beings. As long as we fail to understand what this knowledge is, we'll never be able to distinguish a king with his wisdom from those who merely pretend to be statesmen, but in fact aren't in the slightest, however widely their claim may be believed.[52]

YOUNG SOCRATES: Yes, we already know from earlier stages of the discussion how important this distinction is.

e VISITOR: Now, can a large body of people within a state master this branch of knowledge, do you think?

YOUNG SOCRATES: Of course not.

VISITOR: Suppose a state has a population of a thousand. Could a hundred or even fifty of them become competent statesmen?

YOUNG SOCRATES: If they could, mastering statesmanship would be easier than mastering any other branch of knowledge, because we'd obviously never find that many top-notch *backgammon* players in a population of a thousand people – I mean, people who could match other Greek players – let alone *kings*. I use the plural because, as we've already argued, a person is to be described as a king whether or not he's actually a ruler, as long as he has mastered the branch of

293a knowledge which is kingship.

---

[52] The three intuitive criteria for ranking systems of government are reduced to one – law-abidingness or not – via pressing the question to what degree they embody the expertise of the statesman. This serves to connect this section to the main thread of the argument, since in the process we distinguish more clearly between the true statesman-expert and the people who have the role of rulers in actual states. The question about expertise turns out to favour pressing the criterion of law-abidingness, given the argument of the next few pages that expertise is better than rules and laws, but that laws embodying expertise are a second-best to the expert in person, and far to be preferred than an alternative embodying no expertise at all. The criteria of force, and economic status, are quietly dropped. It emerges that the expert is entitled to employ force and constraint, but no conclusions are drawn as to the role of constraint in the different systems of government. The point about wealth is dropped completely. Aristotle in his own discussion of systems of government (see note 50) thinks this a mistake; indeed

VISITOR: That's a useful reminder. But it follows from what we're saying, surely, that in looking for the phenomenon of perfect rulership, we should be considering a single individual, or two or a very limited number of people, anyway.[53]

YOUNG SOCRATES: Of course.

VISITOR: And it doesn't matter whether they rule by consent or constraint, whether they use or lack a written code, whether they're rich or poor – we still have to regard them as rulers, just as the presence of expertise is the criterion we currently employ to distinguish those who are in charge of any sphere whatsoever. We certainly don't apply or withhold the label 'doctor' depending on whether or not his patients have consented to the treatment, which might b involve surgery or cautery or some other painful procedure, or depending on whether or not he has a written code, or is rich or poor. None of these factors makes the slightest bit of difference: we still call him a doctor, as long as the instructions he issues are guided by expertise, whether he is purging us or otherwise reducing or even increasing our bulk. The only factor we take into consideration is whether the treatment is good for our bodies. We ask only that in tending to our bodies, he is always concerned to preserve them and c improve their condition. Surely it is this factor, and this factor alone, which will make us claim that expertise is the only true criterion for being a doctor and for wielding any other kind of authority.

YOUNG SOCRATES: Absolutely.

VISITOR: The same necessarily goes for political systems too, then, I suppose. The only true system – the political system *par excellence* – is one where it can be shown that the rulers are genuinely and not merely apparently knowledgeable. And by any standard of what constitutes correctness, there's absolutely no need for us to take into consideration whether they rule with or without a legal code, whether or not their subjects have consented to their rule, or whether they d are rich or poor.

he thinks that it is the economic status of the rulers, not their mere numbers, that determines whether a state is a democracy or an oligarchy.

[53] Where does this élitist assumption come from? It is not defended here any more than it is in the *Republic* (it recurs at 297b-c). The analogy with backgammon (admittedly Young Socrates', not the visitor's) is inept; ruling is not like a trivial skill at games, and if the point is meant to be that in any area there are only a few experts, the response is obviously that the number of experts will depend on the area (obviously in a competitive field like games there will only be a few).

YOUNG SOCRATES: Right.

VISITOR: And suppose they purge the state, for its own good, by killing or banishing some of its members; suppose they reduce its size by sending out a bee-swarm of colonists, or increase its size by bringing outsiders in from elsewhere and granting them citizenship. Provided that in doing so they are drawing on their knowledge and their moral sense and are doing their best to preserve the state and improve its condition, then the state still conforms to the factors and
e the criteria which compel us to identify it as having the one and only perfect political system. And we have to say that any other so-called political systems are unreal impostors which merely reflect the one true system and are more or less commendable, depending on how well regulated they are.[54]

YOUNG SOCRATES: On the whole, I find what you've been saying perfectly reasonable, but the idea that one should rule without a legal code strikes a discordant note.[55]

VISITOR: I was just about to ask *you* a question, Socrates; you got
294a yours in first. I was going to ask whether you were happy with everything I'd been saying, or whether there was anything you objected to. But now I see that you'd like us to discuss the matter of how rulers can be true rulers if they lack a legal code.

YOUNG SOCRATES: Of course I do.

VISITOR: Although from one point of view legislation and kingship do certainly go together, the ideal is for authority to be invested not in a legal code but in an individual who combines kingship with wisdom. I wonder if you can see why.

YOUNG SOCRATES: No, why?

VISITOR: Because legislation can never issue perfect instructions
b which precisely encompass everyone's best interests and guarantee fair play for everyone at once. People and situations differ, and human

---

[54] The above passage, with its analogy with the doctor's expertise and frank acceptance of the use of force if expertise is resisted, is very reminiscent of the *Republic*, indeed is probably not fully comprehensible without it. Nothing so far in the dialogue by way of defining the expert ruler's skill has prepared us for this, and Plato is simply relying on the idea that expertise entitles its possessor to constrain the non-expert to do what the expert sees to be required.

[55] This issue is not raised in the *Republic*, where only the ideal state is in question; it arises now because the expert ruler is being compared with systems of government which do proceed by way of law.

affairs are characterized by an almost permanent state of instability. It is therefore impossible to devise, for any given situation, a simple rule which will apply to everyone for ever. I'm sure you agree.

YOUNG SOCRATES: Of course.

VISITOR: But that is obviously exactly what the law aims for. It is like a stubborn, stupid person who refuses to allow the slightest devi- c ation from or questioning of his own rules, even if the situation has in fact changed and it turns out to be better for someone to contravene these rules.

YOUNG SOCRATES: You're right. That's an accurate description of how the law treats us.

VISITOR: Well, it's impossible for something which is unremittingly simple to cope well with things which are never simple, isn't it?[56]

YOUNG SOCRATES: I suppose so.

VISITOR: So why do we feel compelled to make laws, since they can never be entirely successful? We'd better try to discover why. d

YOUNG SOCRATES: Of course.

VISITOR: Now, here in Athens, as in other states, you have ways of training groups of people to excel at running or some other sport, don't you?

YOUNG SOCRATES: Yes, there are a great many methods for that.

VISITOR: Well, let's try to remember the instructions professional trainers give when they're in charge of these groups.

YOUNG SOCRATES: What are you getting at?

VISITOR: They don't find it possible to deal with people selectively, one by one, and to prescribe an appropriate regimen for each individual. Instead, they find they have to prescribe a collective regimen, e one which *usually* benefits *most* people's bodies.[57]

---

[56] The defence of expertise which follows is new and interesting, but it fails to support the point claimed, that expertise entitles the expert to force his remedies on the unwilling non-experts. The rigidity of law faced by changing human circumstances makes Aristotle, in *Nicomachean Ethics* V 10, distinguish between justice, which applies the law, and *epieikeia* (usually translated 'equity'), which applies the spirit of the law in areas where the letter of the law frustrates its original intent because of the rigidity deriving from its necessary generality. Plato's answer is bolder: expertise is always to be preferred to laws, and laws are only even a second-best because they embody the results of expertise.

[57] 'Usually' or 'with the most common situations' (295a) translates *hōs epi to polu*, a phrase prominent in Aristotle, for whom this kind of qualified generalization has an important role.

YOUNG SOCRATES: That's right.

VISITOR: And that's also why they assign to all the members of the group the same amount of exercise. Whatever form of physical exercise is involved – running or wrestling or whatever – they start them all off at the same time, and make them all finish at the same time.

YOUNG SOCRATES: True.

VISITOR: I don't think we should ever expect a legislator either to make his injunctions to his flock in the sphere of morality and 295a human interaction perfectly appropriate to every individual, since he too is issuing instructions for the group as a whole.

YOUNG SOCRATES: Yes, it seems unlikely that he could.

VISITOR: Instead, whether he's issuing written edicts or whether his legislation relies on the unwritten law which consists of time-honoured traditions, his regulations for each community will be rather imprecise and will be concerned, I think, with the majority of the population, with the most common situations, and with being broadly right.

YOUNG SOCRATES: True.

VISITOR: Of course it is, Socrates, because it's impossible to b imagine anyone ever being capable of spending his whole life in close proximity to a given individual, prescribing in minute detail what is appropriate for him. I mean, in my opinion, if anyone with a genuine grasp of kingship were capable of that, he'd hardly complicate things for himself by creating one of these written legal codes we're talking about.

YOUNG SOCRATES: Yes, that certainly follows from what we've been saying.

VISITOR: And it fits even better with the next point, Socrates.

YOUNG SOCRATES: Which is . . .?

VISITOR: I'll tell you. Let's imagine a doctor or a trainer who is c planning a trip abroad and expects to be away from his charges for quite a long time. If he thought that his trainees or his patients would forget his instructions, he'd want to leave written reminders for them, don't you think?

YOUNG SOCRATES: Yes.

VISITOR: But what if his trip didn't last as long as he'd expected? On his return, wouldn't he go about substituting alternative instructions – ones which went against his original instructions – if an alternative course turned out to be better for his patients because some heaven-sent phenomenon or other which he hadn't anticipated d (the wind, for example) had behaved in an unusual fashion? Would he obstinately insist on adherence to his original regulations, and forbid himself from making any new recommendations and any of his patients from daring to act in any way which went against what he'd written down, on the grounds that his original instructions were medically sound and promoted health, whereas if they were changed they'd promote ill health and wouldn't be based on medical expertise? Isn't it rather the case that when such persistent inflexibility is encountered in a man of knowledge, a true professional, it makes the whole enterprise of rule-making look extremely absurd? e

YOUNG SOCRATES: Yes, absolutely.

VISITOR: Now consider the founder of one of the written and unwritten codes which ordain norms of justice and injustice, right and wrong, and good and bad for human beings – or at least for those who are herded together in their various states and are subject to their legislators' codes – and suppose this expert legislator or his double were to return. Is he really not to be allowed to make new regulations which contravene the original code? Isn't the truth of the matter that this prohibition would be just as absurd 296a as the one we mentioned before?

YOUNG SOCRATES: Of course.

VISITOR: You know what the usual position is on this, don't you?

YOUNG SOCRATES: I can't recall it just at the moment.

VISITOR: It's the view – which is certainly plausible – that if a person knows of laws which improve on those of his predecessors, he should get them established, but only once he has persuaded his state to approve them, and not otherwise.

YOUNG SOCRATES: Well, that's right, isn't it?

VISITOR: It may be, but what if force rather than persuasion is b used to improve the constitution? What should we call that kind of force, do you think? Actually, no, don't answer that question yet. Let's start with the case we were looking at earlier.

YOUNG SOCRATES: Which one?

VISITOR: Suppose that, for all his expertise, a doctor fails to persuade someone he's treating, and forces this patient of his (who may not be a child, but an adult man or woman) to follow a better course of action which goes against the instructions he had written out before. What shall we call this kind of force? We're hardly

going to call it an unprofessional defect which will promote ill health, are we? That's the very last thing we'd say. And a patient who has been at the receiving end of this kind of constraint is
c entitled to say anything he likes about it, except that the doctors who forced the treatment on him dealt with him in an unprofessional manner which was liable to promote ill health.[58]

YOUNG SOCRATES: You're absolutely right.

VISITOR: Now, what do we call an defect in statesmanship? Don't we call it an offence, a wrong, a miscarriage of justice?

YOUNG SOCRATES: Exactly.

VISITOR: What about when people have been forced to go against their written code and their traditions, then, and to follow a course of action which is more just, moral and honourable than what they
d were doing before? How is one to react when these people express dissatisfaction with the constraint they've been subjected to? Wouldn't it be the height of absurdity to say that those who applied the pressure treated those who were at the receiving end of it wrongly, unjustly and badly? Wouldn't that be the last thing one should say?

YOUNG SOCRATES: I couldn't agree more.

VISITOR: And is what they're forced to do right if the pressure comes from a rich person and wrong if it comes from a poor person? Isn't it rather the case that whether or not a person gains approval for his measures, whether he is rich or poor, whether he
e adheres to or contravenes the written code, he can still act in their best interests? This is surely where we must find the truest criterion by which to judge whether or not a state is correctly governed; this is the standard a wise and good ruler uses in his management of his subjects' affairs. Here's an analogy. A ship's captain is constantly trying to ensure the best interests of his ship and crew;
297a the way he keeps everyone on board safe is not by giving them written rules to follow, but by making his expertise available to

---

[58] Plato in the *Laws* reverses himself strikingly on this issue, using the same analogy of the doctor, but now to make the point that a free doctor to free people has to *persuade* the patient of the value of the treatment, not just force it on them as does a doctor to slaves (*Laws* 720a-e, 857c-e). Citizens are entitled to demand that they be persuaded of the goodness of a course of action, however expert the rulers.

them – his expertise is their law.[59] It's exactly the same, no different at all, in a state. It is those who are capable of governing in an equivalent way who are the authors of sound systems of government; they make their expertise available, and their expertise is more effective than a legal code. As long as these wise rulers have the single overriding concern of always using their intelligence and expertise to maximize the justice they dispense to the state's inhabi- b tants, there's no defect in what they do, is there? After all, they're not only capable of keeping their subjects safe, but they're also doing all they can to make them better people than they were before.

YOUNG SOCRATES: These ideas of yours are undeniable.

VISITOR: And there's a point that was raised earlier which should also be allowed to stand.

YOUNG SOCRATES: Which one are you talking about?

VISITOR: That it's quite out of the question for a large number of people – never mind who they are – to acquire this knowledge and so govern a state with intelligence. No, if we're to discover the one and only perfect political system we've been talking about, we have to think in terms of scarceness, rarity – uniqueness, even. c And we have to count all other systems as more or less commendable reflections of the true set-up, as we said a short while ago.

YOUNG SOCRATES: Actually, I didn't understand what you meant when you talked about reflection before, so could you explain now?

VISITOR: Of course. It would do no good just to raise the idea and leave it there, without a convincing explanation of where current systems go wrong. d

YOUNG SOCRATES: And where do they go wrong?

VISITOR: Yes, we're going to have to look into this, but it's unfamiliar territory,[60] which makes it hard to investigate. Still, we must try to make sense of it. So ... on the assumption that the political system we've been talking about is the only perfect one,

[59] Another analogy stressed in the *Republic*: see 488a–489d.
[60] Investigation and evaluation of different types of systems of government run according to laws are dismissed as a waste of time in the *Republic* (501a-b) and this is Plato's first attempt at systematic enquiry into it. It is clear from the *Laws* that he proceeded to do a lot of work in this area. Aristotle, with his extensive survey of Greek systems of government, goes much further in this direction.

do you appreciate that other systems have to rely on its written regulations in order to survive? That the course of action they therefore follow is the one which people currently think highly of, although it is not the ideal?

YOUNG SOCRATES: What course of action do you mean?

e VISITOR: Forbidding any member of the state to show the slightest inclination to infringe the laws, and imposing the maximum penalties, up to and including death, on anyone who does dare to do so. Now, there's nothing wrong with this, and it's a perfectly acceptable second-best course of action to fall back on when the ideal we've been discussing has been modified. But do you think we should try to describe how this second-best course, as we called it, starts?

YOUNG SOCRATES: Yes, please.

VISITOR: I think we'd better make further use of the analogies we constantly have to rely on to illustrate the nature of kingship.

YOUNG SOCRATES: What analogies?

VISITOR: Our excellent ship's captain and our doctor 'whose worth is that of many others'.[61] Let's make them the players in an imaginary scenario and see what we discover.

YOUNG SOCRATES: What scenario?

298a VISITOR: I'll tell you. Suppose it was universally believed that they treat people terribly – that although, when they want to, members of both professions keep a person safe and sound, they sometimes choose to injure him. Doctors use surgery and cautery to injure a patient; then they make him pay them a fee (which is their equivalent of taxation) and spend next to nothing on him, but use the bulk of it on themselves and their families; and to cap

b it all they end up by being bribed by their patient's family, or by an enemy of his, and killing him. Then there are sea-captains, with a wide variety of alternative measures at their disposal, whose effect is just the same. Here are just two of their crimes: they enter into conspiracies against people and leave them behind in some deserted spot just as they're about to embark, and they arrange for accidents on the high seas and tip people overboard.

---

[61] The reference to the usefulness of a doctor is from Homer, *Iliad* XI 514–15. Plato is referring to the doctor and ship's captain as stock examples, surely against the background of the *Republic*.

So suppose, since this is our impression of them, that we were to make it a matter of policy that members of these professions are no longer to be allowed unchecked authority over anyone, not c even a slave, let alone a free man. We decide to convene ourselves into an assembly which might either be open to the whole citizen body or be restricted to the wealthier citizens. We make it possible for anyone to voice an opinion about sailing and sickness, whether or not he has any professional knowledge of these or any other occupations. He can suggest how we are to use drugs and medical equipment in treating the sick, and he can also suggest not only what to do with the actual ships, but also how to make use of nautical equipment to cope with seafaring and its risks – some of d which arise just from the fact of being out at sea, subject to wind and water, while others arise from encountering pirates – and whether it is advisable to pit our warships in a naval engagement against other warships.

Once the assembly has heard all this advice, whether it has come from doctors and captains or else from laymen, the majority decision about these matters is written up on the official notice-boards and inscribed on stelae[62] (and also included within the unwritten code consisting of our time-honoured traditions), and from then on it e dictates the ways in which sailing and the treatment of the sick are practised.

YOUNG SOCRATES: You've certainly thought up a strange scenario.

VISITOR: Yes, and it is also our policy, let us suppose, to hold an annual lottery as a means of appointing people (either from among the wealthier citizens or the whole citizen body) to rule over the general populace. Once these rulers have been appointed, they let the written code guide how they direct shipping and heal the sick.

YOUNG SOCRATES: This is even more difficult to take seriously.

VISITOR: But there's a consequence of all this that you also have to consider. Once the rulers' year of office is over, we'll have to

---

[62] The notice-boards referred to are the *kurbeis* or three-sided wooden blocks revolving on a pivot, on which the older laws of Solon were recorded. Later, laws and decrees were recorded on blocks of marble. Plato's reference to the older notice-boards is doubtless meant to point up a contrast between the allegedly haphazard way that political decisions were reached, and their lasting effect.

set up a court and empanel jurors (who can either be selected from among the wealthier citizens or alternatively be chosen by lot 299a from the whole citizen body), and bring the rulers before this court for a review. Anyone who wants to can prosecute any of the rulers for having failed during his year of office to direct shipping in accordance with either our written code or our time-honoured traditions. And the same also goes for those who were responsible for healing the sick. In the case of a guilty verdict, the court decides on the appropriate punishment or fine.[63]

YOUNG SOCRATES: Anyone who voluntarily and of his own free will holds office in circumstances like these deserves any punish-
b ment and fine he gets!

VISITOR: But we haven't finished yet; there's another decree we'll have to enact in addition to all the regulations we've already made. Anyone who is caught looking into how to direct shipping and thinking about seamanship in general, or enquiring into health and trying to discover the true medical position on the effect of climatic factors such as winds and the temperature – whoever develops theories about these matters which go beyond what has been written down in the legal code – is, first, not to be called an expert in medical or naval matters, but a sophist, talking hot air and drivel; second, anyone who is entitled to may, if he wants, bring an indictment against this person and take him to court on the grounds
c that he is corrupting the young people around him and persuading them to engage illegally in naval and medical matters. And if it is decided that he does influence people of any age to behave illegally and in contravention of the written code, then we shall impose the maximum penalty on him, because no one should presume to know more than the law, seeing that anyone who isn't a medical expert with an understanding of health, or a naval expert with an under-standing of commanding ships, can remedy this defect by consulting
d the established written code and traditions.[64]

---

[63] Plato has been presenting as bizarre the standard procedures of the Athenian assembly, ways of appointing to office and scrutiny after office-holding. In the *Laws* his attitude to all of these is more pragmatic and less satirical.

[64] This speech obviously refers bitterly to the trial and execution of Socrates. Cf. *Republic* 488e–489a. It is not very germane to the present point (and what follows in effect ignores it) since Socrates standardly does not claim to be any kind of expert in political matters, although he is represented, at least by Plato, as holding

So, Socrates, suppose this scenario of ours really happened. What would the effect be? Suppose this approach was not restricted to these two branches of knowledge, but was extended to military command and hunting in all its forms, painting and other kinds of representation, carpentry and manufacture of all kinds, and farming and agriculture in general as well. Suppose horse-farming and stock-farming in general were evidently being regulated by a written code, or divination or any other form of service, or backgammon or all the mathematical sciences from straightforward arith- e metic to plane geometry, solid geometry and the study of bodies in motion. If this was how all these branches of knowledge were practised – by reference to a written code and not to expertise – what do you think would happen?

YOUNG SOCRATES: Obviously it would completely obliterate expertise in all its forms, and the ban on research means that there'd be no chance of it ever recurring again either. Life is hard enough as it is, but the effect of all this would be to make life absolutely unbearable in the future.

VISITOR: But here's something else to think about. Suppose all 300a the professions we've mentioned had to conform to written regulations, and we elected (or let a lottery choose) an official to supervise the regulations, but he didn't care about them in the slightest and set about infringing them, not because he knew what he was doing, but perhaps because he'd been bribed, or because he owed someone a personal favour. This would be an even worse state of affairs, wouldn't it, though the previous scenario was bad enough?

YOUNG SOCRATES: You're quite right.

VISITOR: Yes, he'd be infringing the results of a great deal of b experience, I think, and a great deal of clever advice and persuasive argument. That's what it took for the laws to become established, and to go about infringing them would be to commit a far worse error and would undermine all kinds of activities far more effectively than a written legal code.

YOUNG SOCRATES: Of course it would.

VISITOR: And that is why, when laws and statutes *have* been c established (whatever situation they may apply to), the second-best

that there is such a thing as this expertise (at *Gorgias* 521d he claims to be among the few attempting to find it in the right way).

course is to prevent any individual or any body of people from ever infringing them in the slightest.[65]

YOUNG SOCRATES: Right.

VISITOR: Now, these regulations will reflect the truth in their various ways, since they transcribe as accurately as possible what men of knowledge have said.

YOUNG SOCRATES: Of course.

VISITOR: And do you remember what we said before about a man of knowledge, a true statesman? We said that if he saw a course of action which improved on the one he had put into writing and told people to follow while he couldn't be with them, he would d throw away the rule-book and rely on his expertise to guide what he did.

YOUNG SOCRATES: Yes, we did.

VISITOR: So whenever a person or a body of people who do in fact have a code attempt to do something different, something which contravenes this code, they're doing their best to behave just as our true statesman would, aren't they?

YOUNG SOCRATES: Yes.

VISITOR: Doesn't it follow that infringement of law by people who lack knowledge is an attempt – albeit an atrocious attempt – to behave in a way which reflects something authentic, whereas e infringement of law by experts is the absolutely authentic real thing, not a reflection of it?

YOUNG SOCRATES: Definitely.

VISITOR: But we've already established that no large body of people can master any branch of expertise.

YOUNG SOCRATES: Yes, we have.

VISITOR: So – assuming that there is such a thing as expertise at kingship – it cannot be wealthy people collectively or the general

---

[65] Why is the situation presented so starkly? The rigidity of laws, banning flexible application and research into their rationale, is presented as a disaster for expertise, but then upheld absolutely once law is accepted as a second-best political solution. Why does Plato ignore the common-sense position that the rule of law can be constantly modified by a flexible attitude to practice, and improved by ongoing research into its rationale? No argument is given for ignoring this option; Plato seems simply to assume that laws (and traditions) cannot be taken seriously unless they are fixed absolutely; respect for the law precludes fiddling around with it. Cf. 301a. This attitude is seen in even stronger form in the *Laws*.

populace as a whole who have this branch of knowledge, statesmanship, at their command.

YOUNG SOCRATES: Of course not.

VISITOR: States which are governed by these bodies of people
apparently have no choice, then; their only chance of being true
reflections of the authentic political system we've been talking about, 301a
which is government by a single person with expertise, lies in their
never allowing the slightest infringement of their written laws and
their time-honoured traditions, once these have been established.

YOUNG SOCRATES: You're quite right.

VISITOR: Now, the term for a political system which reflects the
one in question and involves government by wealthy people is
'aristocracy', unless they take no notice of the laws, in which case
it is called 'oligarchy'.

YOUNG SOCRATES: That sounds right.

VISITOR: On the other hand, when a single individual who merely
reflects the behaviour of a man of knowledge and never infringes b
the legal code is in power, we call him a 'king', since we don't
have different terms for law-abiding government by a single person,
depending on whether he relies on knowledge or belief.

YOUNG SOCRATES: No, I suppose we don't.

VISITOR: There's no different term, then, even if the single ruler
is a genuinely knowledgeable person: we still use the word and
call him a 'king'. And that's why there are no more than five terms
in all for the systems of government we mentioned earlier.[66]

YOUNG SOCRATES: Yes, I suppose that's why.

VISITOR: What about when a single ruler contravenes both law
and tradition, while making the same claim that our man of know- c
ledge makes – that he has to infringe written law in order to get
the best result – when in fact his reflection of the man of knowledge is being prompted by mere ignorant desire? These are the
circumstances which make us call a single ruler a 'dictator', aren't
they?

YOUNG SOCRATES: Naturally.

VISITOR: So there we have the provenance of dictators, kings,
oligarchy, aristocracy and democracy. These systems are a result

---

[66] Reading δι᾽ ἃ δὴ τὰ πάντα ὀνόματα ... πολιτειῶν πέντε μόνον γέγονεν
(Diès), but keeping the clause at this point in the text.

of discomfort with the kind of government by a single individual that we've been talking about. People doubt that anyone could ever live up to this ideal rulership; they doubt the possibility of a moral and knowledgeable ruler who would dispense justice and deal fairly d with everyone in the matter of their rights; and if such a ruler were possible, they doubt that he would be prepared to rule in that way, rather than injuring and killing and harming any of us whenever he felt like it. And yet, if they were faced with the kind of ruler we're describing, people would feel perfectly comfortable; he'd take sole command of the only system of government which, if we were speaking strictly, we would call authentic, and he'd govern in a way which guaranteed their happiness.[67]

YOUNG SOCRATES: He certainly would.

VISITOR: But what we're saying is that in real life countries aren't e like hives of bees: they don't simply grow a king – an individual whose physical and mental attributes make him stand out from the rest. The only way people can follow the scent of the true political system is apparently by forming assemblies and drawing up written codes.

YOUNG SOCRATES: I suppose so.

VISITOR: So does it come as any surprise, Socrates, to find that these systems are and will continue to be thoroughly rotten, given that they are based on the inadequate foundation of relying on 302a statutes and traditions to guide their actions, when anyone can see that every other branch of knowledge finds that this way of going about things produces disastrous results? Isn't it more surprising to see the inherent strength which states exhibit? I mean, they've been suffering under these systems from time immemorial, but some of them still manage to remain stable and avoid catastrophe. Nevertheless, states do from time to time founder like ships – they often have in the past, and they will continue to do so in the future – as a result of having bad commanders and crew, the

---

[67] The happiness of the ruled emerges somewhat late in the day and is not emphasized. It seems to be assumed, from the *Republic*'s cluster of ideas, that people are happy when they have and do what is best for them, whether this is the result of their own reasoning or not. At 302b we find the idea that what people have in mind is a life under the 'least disagreeable' system of government; Plato continues to think that most ordinary people have a fairly passive view of what is in their own best interests (indeed this is why he attaches such importance to systems of government and their influence).

extent of whose ignorance is matched only by the importance of the matters they are ignorant about. Despite their total ignorance b of statesmanship, they believe that there's no subject which they have mastered more surely and more thoroughly.

YOUNG SOCRATES: This is all too true.

VISITOR: Now, although these flawed political systems all make life difficult, I wonder whether we ought to decide where they stand on a scale from least disagreeable to most oppressive. It may not be strictly relevant to the matter at hand, but it remains the case, generally speaking, that in virtually everything we do we bear this kind of thing in mind.

YOUNG SOCRATES: Yes, I'm sure we ought to decide about this.

VISITOR: On a threefold division of the systems, you'll find that c one of them makes life particularly difficult *and* particularly easy at the same time.

YOUNG SOCRATES: What do you mean?

VISITOR: Just that the three systems we mentioned at the beginning of this argument (which has now burst its banks)[68] were government by a single person, by a limited number of people and by a large number of people.

YOUNG SOCRATES: Yes, that's right.

VISITOR: Well, if we split each of them in two, then we have six, not counting the authentic system which is the seventh.

YOUNG SOCRATES: Can you explain?

VISITOR: Government by a single person generates kingship and d dictatorship; government by a limited number generates the creditable version, aristocracy, and oligarchy; and government by a large number of people generates something which we earlier counted as single and called 'democracy', but now we'd better divide this kind of government as well into two categories.

YOUNG SOCRATES: But how? What criterion do we use?

VISITOR: The same one as usual. The fact that a single term is involved here doesn't make any difference. It's just as possible for there to be law-abiding and law-breaking versions of it as of the e others.

YOUNG SOCRATES: True.

---

[68] An admission that the discussion of systems of government, nominally developed to help distinguish the true expert ruler from competitors, has developed an interest and importance of its own for Plato.

VISITOR: We didn't need to divide it before, when we were trying to discover what the perfect system of government was, because (as we explained at the time) it wouldn't have helped us then. But now we're not taking the perfect system into consideration, and we've found that the others are what we're forced to live with. And the issue of legality and illegality is what divides each of these others into two.

YOUNG SOCRATES: I find this argument of yours quite convincing.

VISITOR: Now when government by a single person is harnessed by adherence to a sound set of stipulations, which we call a legal code, it is the best of the six. When it has no regard for law, however, it is oppressive and makes life difficult.

303a YOUNG SOCRATES: It looks as though you're right.

VISITOR: And I think we should regard government by a limited number of people as occupying the middle position in both the law-abiding and the law-breaking tables, as is suggested by the fact that 'few' falls between 'one' and 'many'. Government by a large number of people is thoroughly feeble, however; compared with the other systems, it is incapable of being an effective force for either good or ill, because under this system authority is broken up into tiny portions and distributed to so many people. That's why it's the worst of all the law-abiding systems, and the best of all the law-breaking ones.

b If no political system restrained its subjects, life in a democracy would take the first prize; if they all did, democracy would be the last one to live in,[69] and the one which would stand out as by far the best is the first one on the list. All this is not counting the seventh system, which we should keep as far apart from all the rest as God is from humankind.

YOUNG SOCRATES: Your conclusions seem to be inescapable. We'd better do as you say.

VISITOR: In that case we'd better dismiss people who are actively
c involved in any of these systems of government except the one which

[69] Plato's revised judgement of democracy is that it is the worst of the three if laws are strictly adhered to, but the best if they are not, for the same reason in each case, namely its extreme division of power. Given that Plato thinks that in the actual world states are meddling with their laws all the time, this is a strongly upward revision of his valuation of democracy from the *Republic*, where it ranks below oligarchy and above only tyranny. The *Statesman* analysis, however, is not only more thoughtful but based on more realistic starting-points, and makes no use of the soul–state analogy; the two dialogues cannot be closely compared on this issue.

is based on knowledge. We should not think of them as statesmen, but as practitioners of sectarian politics. They are agents of a massive sham and are no more than shams themselves; they are supreme impostors and illusionists, they out-sophist the sophists.

YOUNG SOCRATES: It looks as though after a tortuous journey this label 'sophist' has found its true reference – these pseudo-statesmen.

VISITOR: All right, then. It's been just like going to the theatre, hasn't it? We said not long ago that they looked like a roistering band of centaurs and satyrs[70] and that we had to distinguish what they do d from the art of statesmanship, and now we've done so, although it's been far from easy.[71]

YOUNG SOCRATES: Yes, I suppose we have.

VISITOR: Our difficulties are far from over, however. We're left with a group which has more of the properties and qualities of kings, and is therefore harder to distinguish. In fact, I think what's happened to us is pretty much what happens to gold-refiners.

YOUNG SOCRATES: What do you mean?

VISITOR: The first job in that line of work too is, as you know, the removal of earth and stone and plenty of other foreign bodies. After that, they're still faced with a compound, however: there remain a e number of valuable substances which are qualitatively similar to gold and can only be separated from it in a fire – copper, silver and sometimes adamant as well.[72] Removing these substances isn't easy; it takes repeated smelting and application of touchstones, but it's only when they've been removed that we're able to see the proverbial 'pure gold' all by itself, unalloyed.

YOUNG SOCRATES: Yes, I'm told that's what happens.

VISITOR: Well, this seems a good analogy for what we're doing now. We've extracted all the extraneous and incompatible elements from statesmanship, and we're left with those which are valuable and similar. These include expertise in military matters, the administration of justice, and political rhetoric – at least when it cooperates with kingship and helps it in its governmental duties by gaining 304a

[70] Reading Σατυρικόν τινα θίασον with the MSS.

[71] This dismissal of all rulers other than the ideal expert as shams, illusionists and sophists harks back to the *Republic* in its tone, and is surprising after the tone of realism in the previous discussion.

[72] Here and at *Timaeus* 59b 'adamant' is used in a puzzling way. Skemp in his note records a geologist's suggestion that what is meant may be haematite. Later Theophrastus uses the word for diamond.

73

approval for a just course of action. What's the easiest way for us to go about eliminating these fields and letting our quarry, the statesman, be seen purely and simply for what he is in himself?

YOUNG SOCRATES: It should be possible, shouldn't it? We'd better try to find how.

VISITOR: If all it takes is trying, he'll show his face. I think music will help us in our attempt to bring him out of hiding. Here's a question for you.

YOUNG SOCRATES: What?

b VISITOR: Music is a subject, isn't it – something we can learn? And so are all the arts which involve technical proficiency?

YOUNG SOCRATES: Yes.

VISITOR: But what about knowing whether or not we *should* learn any of these subjects? Is this another branch of knowledge which is also concerned with exactly the same subjects, do you think?

YOUNG SOCRATES: Yes, I think we have to say that it is.

VISITOR: And I'm sure we'll agree that it's different from them, won't we?

YOUNG SOCRATES: Yes.

VISITOR: Now, either no branch of knowledge should govern any other branch of knowledge, or the ones we mentioned first

c should govern the other one, or it should govern them. What do you think?

YOUNG SOCRATES: I think it should govern them.

VISITOR: That is, knowing whether or not one should learn a subject ought to govern the subject being learned and taught. Is that your position?

YOUNG SOCRATES: Definitely.

VISITOR: So knowing whether or not persuasion should be used ought to govern knowing how to persuade. Yes?

YOUNG SOCRATES: Of course.

VISITOR: All right. Now, which branch of knowledge do you think

d is responsible for the ability to persuade large numbers of people in a crowd – I mean, by telling them stories rather than by educating them?

YOUNG SOCRATES: The answer seems obvious to me: we have to say it's rhetoric.

VISITOR: And what about knowing whether to use persuasion or some form of constraint on people, or whether to leave them completely alone? Which branch of knowledge is this the province of?

YOUNG SOCRATES: The one which governs the arts of persuasion and speaking.

VISITOR: I suppose you mean statesmanship; I can't think what else you could mean.

YOUNG SOCRATES: Yes, you're quite right.

VISITOR: So it looks as though we've separated rhetoric from statesmanship without too much trouble; we've found that it's a different kind of thing altogether, and is in fact subordinate to states- e manship.[73]

YOUNG SOCRATES: Yes.

VISITOR: Here's another ability to decide about.

YOUNG SOCRATES: What?

VISITOR: Knowing how to conduct a war against people we've declared war on. Is this a matter of expertise, do you think, or not?

YOUNG SOCRATES: Of course it is. How could we think otherwise, when it's what military commanders and strategists do?

VISITOR: What about knowing whether we should go to war, or whether it would be better to settle our differences with our opponents by conciliation? Whose field of competence and knowledge does this fall under? Is it a different branch of knowledge, do you suppose, or the same one again?

YOUNG SOCRATES: We have to say that a different one is involved, otherwise there'll be a clash with earlier conclusions of ours.

VISITOR: And consistency with our previous statements also 305a requires us to maintain that it *governs* military expertise.

YOUNG SOCRATES: I agree.

VISITOR: But military expertise as a whole is such a formidable and important enterprise. What branch of knowledge could we possibly claim it is subordinate to? It could only be true kingship, couldn't it?

YOUNG SOCRATES: Yes.

VISITOR: Since military expertise is a subordinate branch of knowledge, then, we cannot identify it with statesmanship.

[73] In the *Gorgias* it is argued that rhetoric is not an expertise but merely a knack with no rationale. In the *Phaedrus* it is admitted that there is an expertise to the practice of rhetoric, but that it would require philosophy to develop it. Here Plato seems to admit that there is an expertise of rhetoric, which is subordinated to that of ruling and apparently exists in a different person. Plato appears to have reverted to the intuitive viewpoint that there is such a thing as an expertise of rhetoric, and that what matters to the expert ruler is not to deny its existence or to take over its role, but just to ensure that it is used in the right way and for the right ends.

YOUNG SOCRATES: That seems to make sense.

b VISITOR: Now let's see what it is that administrators of justice do, when they do their job correctly.

YOUNG SOCRATES: All right.

VISITOR: Aren't they limited to taking over from the legislator-king all the regulations he has made for human interaction and to deciding questions of legal right and wrong by referring to these regulations? What they bring to the job if they're good at it is the ability to resolve lawsuits between people impartially, without succumbing to bribery

c or threats or tears or any hostile or favourable bias, and so to keep to the legislator's stipulations.

YOUNG SOCRATES: Yes, that's all they do. You've given us a pretty good summary of their job.

VISITOR: So we find, again, that an administrator of justice does not have the power a king has; he is a guardian of the law, and is therefore subordinate to kingship.

YOUNG SOCRATES: So it seems.

VISITOR: When we consider all the branches of knowledge we've mentioned, then, we have to conclude that none of them is identifi-

d able with kingship. The point is that genuine kings do not actually *do* things themselves; they *govern* people whose domain is doing, and they know when to embark on and initiate courses of action which are particularly important to a state, and when it's better to hold back. They delegate action to others.

YOUNG SOCRATES: Right.

VISITOR: And that is why the branches of knowledge we've been discussing don't govern one another, and aren't self-governing either. Each of them has a particular function to perform, and the particular name which is appropriate for it is dictated by that particular function.

e YOUNG SOCRATES: That sounds right.

VISITOR: Then there's the branch of knowledge which is responsible not only for all of them, but for the laws and every other aspect of the state as well, and which creates the best possible fabric out of all these materials. In order to encompass its function, we use a label which all its concerns share and so find that the most appropriate name for it is statesmanship.

YOUNG SOCRATES: Yes, that's absolutely right.

VISITOR: Now that we've seen all the different kinds of materials which go to make up a state, shall we discuss statesmanship in terms of our illustration from weaving?

YOUNG SOCRATES: Yes, I'm sure we should.

VISITOR: So I suppose what we need to describe is what kind of interweaving kings do, how they do it, and what the resulting fabric is like.[74]

YOUNG SOCRATES: Obviously.

VISITOR: These aren't easy matters to explain, but apparently we don't have any choice.

YOUNG SOCRATES: Difficult or not, we have to do it.

VISITOR: The point is that the idea that one aspect of virtue is somehow different from another kind is very easy for argumentative types to attack, given what people usually think about the issue.[75]

YOUNG SOCRATES: I don't understand.

VISITOR: Let me put it this way. I'm sure you believe that courage is one aspect of human virtue.

YOUNG SOCRATES: Yes.

VISITOR: And that self-restraint is also an aspect of human virtue, just as courage is, despite the fact that it's not the same as courage.

YOUNG SOCRATES: Yes.

VISITOR: Now, let's stick our necks out and say something shocking about courage and self-restraint.

YOUNG SOCRATES: What?

VISITOR: That in a sense there's actually a great deal of incompati-

---

[74] The earlier illustration of weaving is now brought back, this time as a metaphor for what the statesman does. This final passage does not strictly add to the official definition, but it expands our understanding of the statesman by showing what he does. Plato needs some such device as this to deal with the question of the statesman's *subjects*, a topic that has surfaced only briefly during the discussion of forms of government. Our grasp of the nature of expert rule cannot be complete until we see what it is exercised on.

[75] The view that the different virtues or types of goodness (*aretai*) are different from one another is common sense, so it is surprising that 'what people usually think' is apparently put on the side of the view that they are not. In the Socratic dialogues many arguments point to the conclusion that what we regard as different virtues are merely different patterns or areas of behaviour which exemplify a single state, practical knowledge of an expert kind, which is applied in all of them. The question whether the different virtues imply one another (the reciprocity of virtue) or are taken to be just one and the same state (the unity of virtue) is left unresolved. What we find here seems to be a rejection of any version of this view, but the issue is in fact somewhat complex. For detailed analysis of the passage see Bobonich.

bility between them, and that there are plenty of contexts in which they directly conflict with each other.

YOUNG SOCRATES: What are you saying?

VISITOR: Something very unusual, since the common view is that
c every aspect of virtue is compatible with every other aspect.[76]

YOUNG SOCRATES: Yes, it is.

VISITOR: I think we should look into the matter extremely carefully. Is it as simple as the usual view says, or is it rather the case that occasionally they can somehow be at odds with each other, despite belonging to the same family?[77]

YOUNG SOCRATES: Yes, I'm sure we should look into this, but can you tell us how?

VISITOR: The phenomenon we're looking for can be found all over the place, wherever there are qualities which we regard as desirable, but still count as opposites.

YOUNG SOCRATES: Can you give a clearer explanation, please?

VISITOR: Consider liveliness and speed. It doesn't matter whether
d you think of them as physical or mental or vocal, and it doesn't matter whether you think of them in themselves or as portrayed impressionistically by musicians and by painters, of course. Have you yourself ever approved of these qualities, or has anyone else ever done so in your hearing?

YOUNG SOCRATES: Naturally.

VISITOR: And do you remember how approval is always phrased in these cases?

YOUNG SOCRATES: No, I don't.

VISITOR: I wonder whether I'll be able to explain my ideas to you.
e YOUNG SOCRATES: Why shouldn't you?

VISITOR: You seem to think we're talking about something simple. Anyway, let's look at some opposites and see if they help us understand the issue. Here's an example. There are plenty of events and occasions when we welcome speed, energy and liveliness (whether they're occurring in a mental, physical or even vocal form), yet there's

---

[76] Note that the issue has shifted; what most people think is now not that all parts or aspects of virtue are unified, but merely that they are compatible with one another, a clearly weaker view.

[77] This could show that in different situations diverse factors bring the exercise of one virtue into conflict with the exercise of another; but this falls short of showing that the virtues themselves are such that there can be a conflict between them. Plato does not distinguish these possibilities.

just the one concept we invariably rely on to express our approval, and that is 'courage'.

YOUNG SOCRATES: What do you mean?

VISITOR: We couple 'lively' with 'bold', for instance, and 'swift' with 'spirited', and 'energetic' with something similar. In short, we express our approval of things with these qualities by talking about them all equally in terms of the attribute I've mentioned.

YOUNG SOCRATES: Yes.

VISITOR: However, there are also plenty of contexts in which we 307a approve of doing things calmly, aren't there?

YOUNG SOCRATES: There certainly are.

VISITOR: And isn't our approval couched in terms which contradict the ones we use for the other set of qualities?

YOUNG SOCRATES: What do you mean?

VISITOR: For instance, when we're expressing approval of steady, gentle thoughts and actions, or of an even, measured tone of voice, or of rhythmic movement and music in general when they're as unhurried as the occasion demands, we use the terms 'quiet' and 'restrained', as you know. We never talk about them in terms of b courage, but in terms of composure.

YOUNG SOCRATES: You're absolutely right.

VISITOR: But when either set of qualities doesn't suit the occasion, we criticize them instead, in terms which contradict the way we speak when we're approving of them.

YOUNG SOCRATES: What do you mean?

VISITOR: We describe inopportune liveliness and speed, or an unduly strident voice, as violent and frantic; an unsuitably measured tone of voice, on the other hand, or excessive slowness and gentle- c ness, we call timid and sluggish. It's more or less true to say that these defects, as well as the self-restraint and courage which are opposed to them, are in a manner of speaking categories which are separated by mutual hostility and conflict, so that we never find the two of them together in any relevant activity. And with further reflection we'll see that people with these characteristics are at odds with one another as well.

YOUNG SOCRATES: What might lead us to see this?

VISITOR: We don't need to look any further than the cases we mentioned a moment ago (although I'm sure there are plenty of others too), because it's their own affinity with one or the other d set of qualities which makes people approve of things they feel are congenial and familiar, and disapprove of the alternatives, which they feel are foreign: this is what makes people quarrel so bitterly with one another over all sorts of issues.[78]

YOUNG SOCRATES: Yes. I think you're probably right.

VISITOR: Now, when the conflict between the two categories occurs in the human sphere like that, it remains trivial; but when it occurs in serious contexts, there's nothing which poses a worse threat to the health of states.[79]

YOUNG SOCRATES: What are these serious contexts?

e VISITOR: I mean everything which makes life possible, as you might expect. You see, people who are particularly self-contained always like to live a quiet life, keeping themselves to themselves and looking after their own affairs; that's how they deal with everyone at home, and by the same token they like to find a way to be on peaceful terms with other states abroad. And because they don't restrict this love of theirs only to suitable contexts, then, when they get their own way in politics, they imperceptibly make the younger generation just as incapable of waging war as they themselves are, until they're at the mercy of any and every aggressor. The consequence of all this is that, before too many years have passed, they themselves and their children and the whole state might

308a well have exchanged freedom for slavery, without even realizing it.

YOUNG SOCRATES: That's awful – a dreadful thing to happen.

VISITOR: But what about people whose bias is towards courage? Aren't they constantly working their community up into a state of warlike intensity, because of their excessive enthusiasm for the military life? This leads them to make a great many powerful enemies, and consequently they cause their homeland either to be completely destroyed or, again, to be plunged into a state of slavery and submission to their enemies.

---

[78] The analogy with vigour and restraint suggests that all that is in play are tendencies in human characters which can, when unchecked, lead to undesirable extremes. These tendencies are not in themselves virtues (which require a reflected ability to discern the right thing to do) any more than vigour and restraint are, and so Plato seems mistaken in saying that we have actual virtues which are incompatible.

[79] Plato is concerned in all three of his political dialogues to achieve a certain kind of citizen character which is neither too aggressive nor too feeble. He is aware of the need to have citizens who can defend themselves and their state, but he also wants to avoid militarism of the Spartan kind. This passage foreshadows the thorough and extreme measures in the *Laws* to create a citizen body with the

YOUNG SOCRATES: Yes, that's true. b

VISITOR: It's undeniable that in these contexts we find our two categories constantly involved in bitter conflict and serious hostility with each other, isn't it?

YOUNG SOCRATES: Yes, definitely.

VISITOR: So we've discovered the answer to the question we started with, haven't we? These two important parts of virtue[80] are inherently at odds with each other, and as human characteristics they have the same effect on people.

YOUNG SOCRATES: Yes, I'm sure you're right.

VISITOR: Here's the next point to consider, then.

YOUNG SOCRATES: What?

VISITOR: Whether any line of work which involves the manufac- c
ture of items by combining different materials chooses to use both poor and good materials to make even the most insignificant of its products. Isn't it the case, rather, that every branch of knowledge, whatever its province, does all it can to avoid poor materials and accepts only good, useful ones? And that it combines all these materials (whether they are similar or dissimilar to one another) into a single product with a single function and form?

YOUNG SOCRATES: Of course.

VISITOR: The same goes for true statesmanship, then, as well. d
No authentic statesman will ever choose to use both good and bad people as his materials for constructing a state. It's patently obvious that he'll start by testing their soundness during their childhood games, and then (if they pass the test) he'll put their education in the hands of the experts – people who can serve him in this capacity. He supervises the educators, though, and gives them their instructions, just as a weaver personally directs and supervises the carding and every aspect of the preparation of the things he'll need for his weaving, and makes sure that all his assistants know what he wants them to do in order to contribute towards the fabric he e
has in mind.[81]

---

virtues of warriors when required, but with cooperative and peaceful temperaments where political matters are concerned.

[80] But in the previous speech they were described simply as 'categories' (*genos*, a more general term than *eidos*), i.e. part of the material for virtue, not virtue itself.

[81] This passage presupposes a system of totally organized education and upbringing which the citizens receive. Plato stresses the ethical importance of early play in both the *Republic* and the *Laws*.

YOUNG SOCRATES: I agree.

VISITOR: I'd say that a king treats all the official educators and instructors in his state in exactly the same way. In his supervisory role, which he retains for himself, he doesn't allow them to use any forms of training except those which will result in a character which will suit the synthesis he's trying to achieve, and these are the only people he lets them teach. As for other kinds of people – well, first there are those who are capable of acquiring courage, self-restraint and other moral tendencies, and who are driven by their evil dispositions to violate the dictates of religion, justice and morality. In their case, he uses death and exile and the most degrading forms of punishment to rid the state of them.

YOUNG SOCRATES: Yes, that's what people suggest should happen.

VISITOR: However, he demotes to slavery those who are stuck in the depths of mean-spirited ignorance.[82]

YOUNG SOCRATES: Right.

VISITOR: Then there are the rest – those who have the potential for being men of calibre if they are properly educated and who are capable of accepting the process by which a skilled craftsman blends them into a society. Some of them incline towards courage and have a solidity of character which the statesman thinks of as his warp; the others incline towards restraint and, in the terms of our analogy, he thinks of them as forming the less compact, soft thread of the weft, and uses them as such. He takes these two opposite tendencies and tries to find a way to link and weave them together.

YOUNG SOCRATES: How?

VISITOR: In accordance with the principle of affinity. He first harmonizes the eternal parts of their minds by linking them to one another in a divine manner, and then afterwards uses human bonds to harmonize their mortal aspect.

YOUNG SOCRATES: I don't understand what you're saying again.

VISITOR: When a person has, and securely has, true beliefs about right and wrong, justice and injustice, and good and bad, then –

---

[82] A new idea; in both the *Republic* and the *Laws* Plato treats slavery as an unavoidable but morally arbitrary fact of life, something outside the sphere of justice brought about by the expert ruler.

since beliefs occur in people's minds – this is a manifestation of divinity in a divine medium.[83] That's what I'm saying.

YOUNG SOCRATES: Yes, that sounds plausible.

VISITOR: Do you appreciate that it is only a statesman, an expert d on law and convention, who has the right and the ability to draw on the Muse of kingship and instil these truths in people – provided they've received a proper education, as we said a moment ago?

YOUNG SOCRATES: That seems to make sense.

VISITOR: And we should deny any and all of the titles we're investigating to people who lack this ability, Socrates.

YOUNG SOCRATES: Quite right.

VISITOR: Now, there's no better way for a courageous person to become civilized and to admit morality into his life than for him to e become convinced of these truths, is there? Without them, however, he degenerates towards bestiality, doesn't he?

YOUNG SOCRATES: Of course.

VISITOR: What about a self-contained person? Doesn't he gain genuine self-restraint and sound judgement – or at any rate, as much as he needs to function within a society? Without them, however, doesn't he get vilified, quite rightly, as a simpleton?

YOUNG SOCRATES: Yes.

VISITOR: Now, it's quite out of the question for there to be any stable interweaving or linking of bad people with one another, or of good with bad, isn't it? No branch of knowledge would make any serious effort to work with these combinations of people, would it?

YOUNG SOCRATES: Of course not.

VISITOR: This interweaving can only take place, guided by law, 310a between people who are born with a good disposition which is then fostered in their upbringing. It is a skilfully prescribed corrective for these people – in other words, it is what we described as the more divine of the two ways of linking together aspects of virtue

---

[83] Shared true belief about moral and political matters is here described in more elevated terms than hitherto. In the *Republic* it is important, but not described as anything divine. The citizens' true belief is still, however, here made directly dependent on the expert ruler's knowledge, as in the *Republic*; Plato has not yet moved to the *Laws* view that the citizens' virtue, and exercise of the divine in us, lies in understanding and conforming to laws and traditions.

which are in themselves dissimilar and tend in opposite directions.[84]

YOUNG SOCRATES: You're quite right.

VISITOR: Now, once the divine link is in place, it's not particularly difficult to envisage the remaining links, the human ones, or to translate the ideas into reality, either.

b YOUNG SOCRATES: What do you mean? What are these human links?

VISITOR: I'm thinking of the ones formed by intermarriage, by alliances between children from the two groups, and by the alliances which result from one group arranging for its daughter to marry into the other group. As far as procreation is concerned, these links are usually formed in the wrong way.

YOUNG SOCRATES: Why?

VISITOR: Well, people either use them to pursue wealth and power – but I don't see any reason even to criticize this practice. It would just be a waste of breath.

YOUNG SOCRATES: I quite agree.

VISITOR: But others make people's character their chief concern,
c and this does deserve our attention, if there's something wrong with the way it's done.

YOUNG SOCRATES: Yes, I suppose so.

VISITOR: Well, in fact, there isn't a single sound thought behind the way people go about it. They just do whatever it's easy for them to do in their current situation. They like people who are similar to themselves and dislike people who aren't; if they don't feel comfortable with people, they count that as extremely important.

YOUNG SOCRATES: What do you mean?

VISITOR: I'm sure you've noticed that self-contained people search
d out others who simply mirror their own character. The men do all they can to marry women from families of the same type, and fathers too are always trying to marry their daughters into families of the same type. Courageous people do exactly the same: they chase after their own temperament. In fact, though, both groups ought to be doing exactly the opposite.

[84] Real virtue is produced primarily by the 'divine bond' of correct beliefs about right and wrong; this is what checks the two temperaments which when unchecked go to extremes. Thus despite Plato's earlier wording there is no real conflict among the virtues themselves. The idea here has obvious affinities to the earlier thoughts on the mean as the corrective of excess and deficiency, but Plato does not apply those ideas here himself.

YOUNG SOCRATES: What do you mean? Why should they?

VISITOR: Because if courage is reproduced in generation after generation without being diluted by restraint, then what begins as vigour and energy ends by running riot as complete insanity.

YOUNG SOCRATES: I suppose you're right.

VISITOR: On the other hand, when a temperament which has more than its share of modesty, and no trace of spirit and courage, is e perpetuated in this fashion for a number of generations, it becomes excessively indolent and, eventually, completely incapacitated.

YOUNG SOCRATES: Yes, again I suppose so; that must be what happens.

VISITOR: These alliances are the links I was saying wouldn't be at all hard to form once both types of people were already unanimous about moral matters. The point is that the only task the weaver-king has to do, the sum total of his work, is to ensure that restrained and courageous characters never drift apart; he has to weave them together by having them share beliefs, respect and disrespect the same qualities, and betroth their children to one another. He has to form them into an even and, we might say, well-textured fabric, and never allow positions of power in the state to be held by one or the 311a other type exclusively.

YOUNG SOCRATES: How will he achieve this?

VISITOR: Wherever he finds an office that needs only a single administrator, he'll choose someone who combines both qualities; wherever more than one person is needed, he'll form his committee from a combination of both types. You see, when restrained people are in power, they're very careful, fair and conservative, but they lack incisiveness and a certain driving energy and effectiveness.

YOUNG SOCRATES: Yes, I agree to that too.

VISITOR: Whereas when courageous people are in power, they're b less fair and cautious than the others, but have far more drive to get things done. In any state, it takes the presence of both these qualities at once for anything – an individual's personal business or a public state matter – to prosper.

YOUNG SOCRATES: Of course.

VISITOR: What we're saying, then, is that the work of a weaver-statesman is complete when he has woven these two types of human character – the courageous and the restrained – into a tight fabric. It is complete when a king with his knowledge makes sure that conc sensus and loyalty are the materials out of which he constructs their communal life, and so creates the most magnificent and excellent fabric there can be – a seamless cloth in which he enfolds all his subjects, whether slave or free – and when his rule, his government, is such that it maximizes to the fullest degree the potential a state has for attaining happiness.

YOUNG SOCRATES: You're quite right.

SOCRATES: Thank you, my friend. You've done a wonderful job of fully describing the statesman-king for us.[85]

---

[85] Only the last passage moves from characterizing the nature of the statesman's ability to rule to illustrating its connections with running the state and with making its citizens happy, and these connections are brought out only briefly and elliptically. They make it clear that Plato still thinks that a well-governed state will produce consensus of thought and feeling on basic moral issues, by means of a total education of character from the earliest years. Only in the *Laws* does Plato go on to link this closely with the new interest in non-ideal systems of government that has emerged in the *Statesman*. The present rather lame ending is one sign that Plato has not yet successfully integrated these two concerns. He does not do so until he gives up the *Statesman*'s focus on the ideal ruler.

Index

Index

Cambridge Texts in the History of Political Thought

Titles published in the series thus far